Play by the Rules

Play by the Rules

CREATIVE PRACTICE IN DIRECTION-FOLLOWING

By Greta Rasmussen

ISBN 0-936110-09-0
Library of Congress Catalog Card Number: 89-051969

TIN MAN PRESS
BOX 219
STANWOOD, WA 98292

Contents

Introduction

This is an unusual book. It is inventive and full of surprises. Each of the activities in "Play by the Rules" is highly original — designed specifically for the purpose of sharpening listening and direction-following skills. You'll find no silly instructions to color bunny ears pink or squirrel tails brown here! Rather, you will encounter all sorts of unexpected challenges, ranging from instructions which will produce extremely sophisticated designs to listening games guaranteed to keep children on the edges of their seats.

Although the spirit of fun — of play — sets the personality of this book, there is a serious purpose. Good listening and direction-following skills are vital to a child's success in the classroom. As our society becomes more complex, they are becoming increasingly vital to success in adult life, also. This is particularly true in terms of spoken (as opposed to written) directions. It is a fact of modern life that we are receiving more and more of our information through electronically-transmitted speech... by telephone or through radio and TV. During one recent seven-year period, for example, the time Americans spent on the telephone increased by 24 percent, while the population grew at a rate of just seven percent. And of course we're all aware of the amount of time spent in front of the TV or tuned in to the radio.

This book meets a real (and growing) need, therefore. We feel it represents an important step forward in the development of the kind of critical listening and direction-following skills your students need to acquire.

You will notice that we have made an attempt to vary both the length and the level of difficulty of the activities. The book begins with a series of three "warm-up" exercises designed to provide some practice in the various types of instructions children will be encountering. It then continues with a number of relatively simple challenges. But the simplicity does not last for long, for very quickly children will be producing some highly complex responses as they follow your directions.

Since all of the activities involve information which you will be presenting orally, we have provided what amounts to a script for you to follow. Of course, there will be times when your own words and style will be better. However, the instructions have been so carefully structured that very little "ad libbing" should be necessary.

Speaking of structure, it is very important that you set up some firm guidelines regarding children's behavior during these exercises. Stress that although the activities will be a lot of fun, they *must* be done according to *your* rules. For example, don't allow children to ask for instructions to be repeated over and over again. Let them know from the start that it is their responsibility to listen carefully if they want to "play." To make sure you are firmly in charge, it would probably be a good idea for you to run through each of these activities yourself ahead of time. Or, you might wish to try them out on a friend or colleague.

You will notice that we have provided a number of typical "solutions" to the challenges you will be presenting. Be sure to take a glance at them before you launch in. You will also note that most of the activities require very little advance preparation. In some instances we ask you to provide a simple worksheet which you will need to draw and duplicate, but keep in mind that your squares, rectangles and circles don't have to be perfect. Also, you will occasionally need some "props," such as soda crackers, bread slices, paper clips, etc. The children themselves will require nothing more than a pencil and occasionally crayons, a ruler or scissors. We have tried to keep things simple!

One word of caution. It will always be very important to emphasize to students that they are to react only after you have spoken the entire direction. Students who jump into an activity too soon will be sorry!

So there is some serious work ahead. But the fun of this book — the play — should not be minimized. We think there is enough of that to make these activities highly motivational. The children we worked with as we were developing "Play by the Rules" had great fun with challenges such as "The Triangle-ope," in which they were asked to draw an imaginary animal in response to a make-believe explorer's written account. But we expected that. What surprised us was the amount of fun they had with the tougher activities, such as "Build a Message." They seemed to take real delight in the realization that they were capable of meeting some very complex challenges simply by listening carefully and taking one step at a time.

In short, we feel this book offers a fresh and effective approach to the teaching of listening and direction-following skills. We know it contains activities you will not find anywhere else... of that much we're sure, because we had the fun of inventing them! We hope you will find this book enjoyable to use and that your students will benefit as they learn to PLAY BY THE RULES!

Warm-Ups (1)

About this activity...

This book begins with three introductory activities designed to acquaint students with some of the direction-following processes they will be encountering. Handle this first activity casually, using the "friendly" faces as a comfortable way to get started.

Materials needed...

Plain paper, pencil.

Directions to students...

How carefully do you listen? How well do you follow directions? Today, we are going to start some listening and direction-following activities which should be a lot of fun.

If you don't understand a direction, just raise your hand and I will repeat it. But I will never repeat a direction more than twice. That means you must pay attention.

One warning: It is important that you always listen to the whole direction before you make any marks on your paper. I will always pause after giving you a direction, so there will be plenty of time for you to do what I have asked.

For our activity today, we're going to draw six faces. We're going to begin in a very simple way — by drawing six ovals. Then, it will be up to you to follow my instructions to turn the ovals into six faces. Let's get started.

- First, draw six ovals. Draw them so they almost fill up the sheet of paper. You can arrange them in any way you wish.
- Now, I want you to number your ovals 1-6. Put the numbers directly under the ovals.
- It's time now to make some faces! Start by giving Number 1 eyes, a nose, a mouth, ears and hair. Draw fairly quickly, because we have a lot to do.
- Next, I want you to give Number 2 a smile... just a smile.
- Now, give Number 6 a frown.
- Give Number 4 two letter "O's" for eyes.
- Give Number 3 an upside-down number "7" for a nose.
- How about Number 5? Let's start with some very small ears. Give it a small mouth, a very small nose, and very small eyes.

- Give Number 2 a very big nose. Give it curly hair, also.
- Now, let's go back to Number 3. I want you to give it two dots for eyes, and two upside-down letter "V's" for eyebrows.
- Why is Number 6 mad? Because it has a bee sitting on it! Draw a bee — not the letter, the insect — on top of Number 6's head.
- Now, give Number 6 a nose. Give that same face some eyes that are looking up at the bee.
- Give Number 2 a pair of triangles for eyes.
- Number 3 is tired! Give it a mouth that is yawning.
- Well, let's see. What about Number 4? Please give Number 4 a letter "U" for a nose and then give it a mouth that is just a straight line.
- Now, the last thing I want you to do is this: I want you to make it look like Number 4 is looking at the bee on the head of Number 6.

Sadie Boge, age 10

DON'T ALLOW CHILDREN TO ADD ADDITIONAL DETAILS. (THAT WAY YOU CAN SEE AT A GLANCE WHETHER OR NOT THEY HAVE FOLLOWED DIRECTIONS.)

Warm-Ups (2)

About this activity...

This activity is pure "meat-and-potatoes" direction-following and may be a bit frustrating to those students who want everything they do to "look like something." Just tell them, "I took you on a long, roundabout journey and you all ended up in about the same place. Isn't that neat?"

Materials needed...

Plain paper, pencil.

Directions to students...

Ready for another direction-following activity? Remember, we made six faces last time. Well, today we are going to try something different. Today, we will not be making a picture of something; we will just be making some interesting marks for practice. Let's get started and you'll see what I mean.

- First, I want you to fold your paper in half by bringing the top and bottom edges together. Press down on the fold to make the crease sharp.
- Next, keeping the paper folded, fold the paper in half again, with the fold going the other way this time. Press down on the fold, and then open up the paper and smooth it out.
- You should have four rectangles that were made by folding the paper. Place the paper so that one of the short sides is closest to you.
- Now, draw a big circle in each one of the rectangles. Try to fill up as much of the rectangle as you can. Since you are drawing your circles by hand, they won't be perfect. Don't worry.
- Look at the space in the middle of the paper between the four circles. Draw another circle in that space. If you can do it, make the middle circle touch the edges of the other circles.
- Now, I want you to number the five circles. Put the numbers under the circles, just outside the bottom edge. Number the circle at the top left "1." The circle on the top right will be "2." The middle circle is "3." The circle on the bottom left is "4." The circle on the bottom right should be numbered "5."

Now, I am going to give you 20 directions. I will go fairly quickly, so listen carefully.

- Make a small circle about the size of a penny in the middle of Circle 2.
- Make a small triangle in the middle of Circle 5.
- Write a capital letter "X" in the middle of Circle 4.
- Draw a small square in the middle of Circle 1.
- Draw a straight line all the way across Circle 3. It should go straight across, not up and down.

- Draw another larger circle around the small circle you drew in Circle 2.
- Continue the lines of the "X" you drew in Circle 4 all the way out to the edge of the circle.
- Draw a straight line between the middle of the square in Circle 1 and the middle of the smallest circle in Circle 2.
- Make a black dot at each corner of the triangle in Circle 5.
- Use one more line to turn the mark you made in Circle 3 into a big plus sign.
- Look at the line between Circles 1 and 2. If part of the line is outside of the circles, erase it.
- Make a bigger triangle around the small triangle you made in Circle 5.
- Draw another line from the center of Circle 4 out to the edge of the circle. Make sure it doesn't touch any of the lines that are already in the circle.
- Think of Circles 3 and 4 as pizzas. How many separate pieces have you made? Write that number somewhere in Circle 5.
- Turn the number you just made in Circle 5 into a four-leaf clover.
- Use four straight lines to connect the ends of the plus sign you made in Circle 3.
- Put a small circle at each of the corners of the square in Circle 1. Put the small circles outside, not inside, the corners.
- Put an "X" inside each of the triangles you have made in Circle 3.
- Connect the end of the line inside the small circle in Circle 2 with the top point of the triangle in Circle 5.
- Relax, you are finished! Write your name in the bottom section of Circle 4.

AN EXAMPLE OF A COMPLETED PROJECT. FOLDS ARE INDICATED BY THE DOTTED LINES.

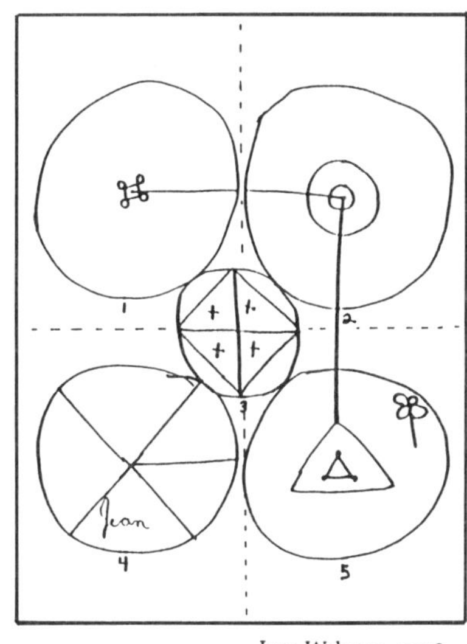

Jean Webster, age 9

Warm-Ups (3)

About this activity...

In this assignment, children are asked to build a design by following simple, step-by-step directions. It should come as a revelation that something so complex can be achieved by working through such a simple set of procedures. The coloring aspect is a bonus to make the end result more satisfying.

Materials needed...

Plain paper, pencil, crayons.

Directions to students...

We are going to be making an interesting design for today's direction-following activity.

- Your first job is easy. Draw a big circle in the middle of your paper. Try to make it as large as you can without touching the edges of the paper. Since you will be making the circle by hand, it won't be perfect. That's okay. Also, it doesn't matter whether the short or the long side of the paper is in front of you. Just draw the big circle and do the best you can.

Does everyone have a circle? All right, now follow these directions carefully.

- Make three dots somewhere inside the circle. Space them out and do not put them in a straight line.

- Make three more dots on the line that forms the circle. Do not put the dots too close together, but do make sure they touch the line that forms the circle.

- Draw straight lines to connect the three dots that are inside the circle. Since you are not using a ruler, your lines will not be perfectly straight, but that's all right.

- Draw straight lines between the three dots that are on the edge of the circle. It doesn't matter if the lines cross lines you have already made.

- Now, draw straight lines between all of the dots that you have not connected so far.

- Find the largest shape you have made that has one curved edge and put a dot somewhere in it.

- Find the largest shape you have made that has three straight sides and put a dot somewhere in it.

- Draw a straight line to connect the two dots you have just made.

- Add four more straight lines between the two new dots and any of the other dots. Put them wherever you think they will help to make your design more interesting.

Now, get out your crayons.

- Color in all of the shapes that have curved sides with a yellow crayon.
- Use a red crayon to color in two of the shapes that have three straight sides.
- Use a blue crayon to color in the shapes that have more than three straight sides.
- Finally, use your pencil to print your first name inside one of the uncolored shapes.

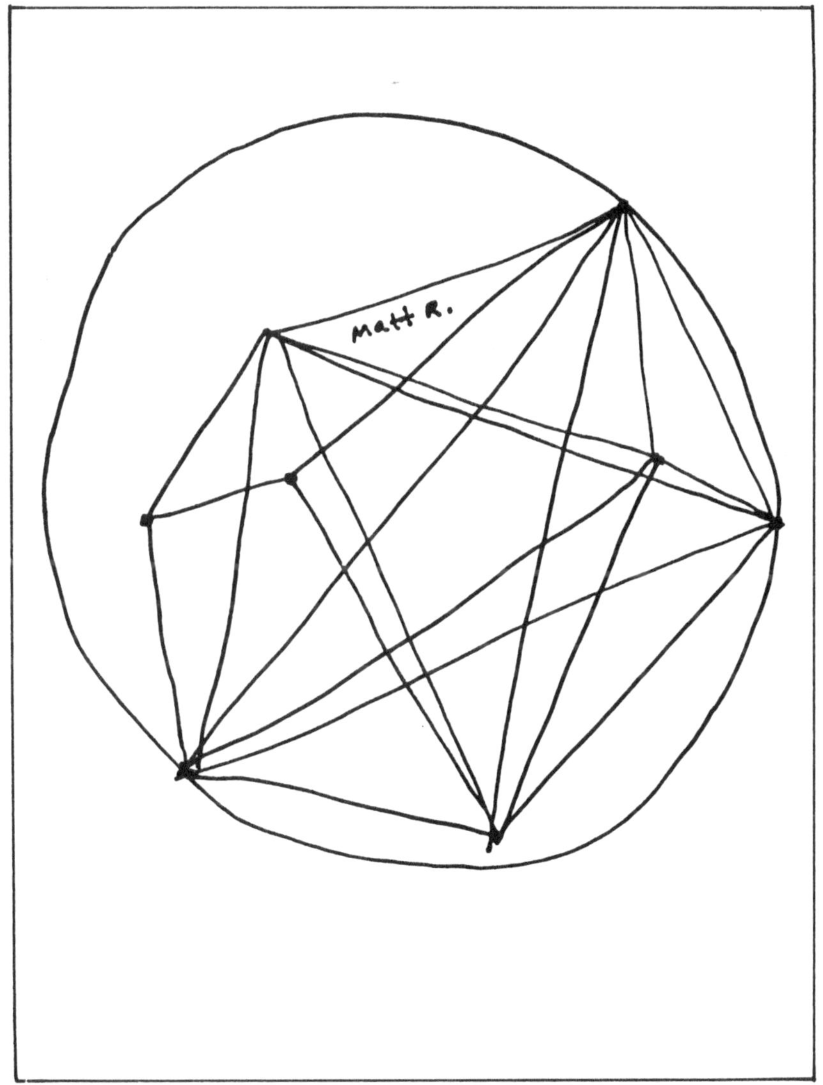

Matt Roberts, age 10

NOTE: STUDENT'S COLOR CHOICES NOT SHOWN.

Letter Tricks

About this activity...

Children love the circus. So why not turn letters into circus performers? This activity asks children to visualize how letters would look as they put together their balancing act.

Materials needed...

Plain paper, pencil.

Directions to students...

A lot of letters got together on the playground one day and decided they would invent a neat circus act. "Let's do a balancing act," said the letters. "Let's try to make a really high stack of letters without falling down."

In our activity today, which is called "Letter Tricks," we're going to find out what the letters did to put together their balancing act.

I have given you a long, skinny piece of paper. Begin by putting one of the short sides of the paper closest to you. Next, draw a line all the way across the paper, about an inch from the bottom. Let's pretend the line is the ground. That's where the bottom letter in the balancing act will be standing.

There are a couple of rules. All of the letters you will be drawing should be capitals, and they should be about an inch tall.

All right. Listen carefully and we'll see how our letters are going to perform their act.

- First came an X. The X said, "I stand on two feet and I'm very strong, so I'll be on the bottom." Okay, now draw the X on the ground line.
- "I have two legs, too," said an M. "I'll stand with the bottom of my legs resting on the top of your arms." And so the M climbed up on the X. Show how that would look.
- Next, an O said, "Since I'm round, I can fit a little way down into the top of the M. That will keep me from rolling off." So up went the O. Show the O up on top of the M.
- Now it was W's turn. "If I put my two bottom points on top of the O, I can balance there without falling off," said the W. Show how the W would look on top of the O.
- "My turn," said a Q. "Since I look a lot like an O, I think I can balance on the W the way the O is balancing on the M." Everyone agreed that the Q was right, so it climbed up. Draw the Q.
- N's turn came next. "Since I stand on one leg and one point, I think I can stand up on top of the Q," said the N. The N climbed up. Go ahead and show us how that would look.

- "I'm not afraid of high places," said an E. "If I lie down on my back I can balance on top of the N very well." So E climbed up and rested on its back. Show how that would look.
- All of the letters which were still on the ground looked up at the E, which had all three of its arms sticking straight up in the air. They agreed that the next letter in the stack should be a Z, which could rest its long bottom line across the E's arms. Show the Z up on top of the E.
- "Let me be next," said an A. "I have two good legs and I'll be able to stand on top of the Z very well." So up climbed A. Show how that would look.
- Now the letters really had a problem. How could anyone balance up on top of the point of the A? The Y looked up at the A, which was very high up in the air, and said, "I have been standing on one leg all my life. I'm sure I can balance on the point of the A." So the Y climbed up and, sure enough, it was able to balance very well.

Were you all able to show how the letters looked for their circus act? Let's see how you did.

CUT A PIECE OF 8½" x 11" PAPER IN HALF VERTICALLY FOR THIS PROJECT.

Brenna Woiwod, age 7

12 Circles

About this activity...

This activity asks youngsters to think about a basic shape — the circle — in a creative, flexible manner.

Materials needed...

Worksheet (see illustration), pencil.

Directions to students...

Today, we're going to be doing an activity called "12 Circles." When we are finished, all of the circles will have been changed into something else. Listen carefully, and try to do exactly what I tell you to do.

- Change Circle 3 into a doughnut by drawing just one small circle.
- Put a dot in the middle of Circle 10. Then, draw eight straight lines to make it look something like a bicycle wheel.
- Do anything you wish to Circle 7 to make it look like the head of an owl.
- What time is it right now? Turn Circle 4 into a clock with its hands pointing to the time it is now. You don't have to put in the numbers.
- What can you do to Circle 2 to make it look something like an apple? Do it now.
- What do most people like on their French fries? Some people like catsup, of course, but almost everyone likes a little salt. Do something to Circle 5 to make it look like the top of a salt shaker.
- You and three of your friends are going to share a pizza. Use Circle 1 to show how you could give everyone an equal share by making just two cuts.
- What is the easiest way to make Circle 8 look like a button? You decide, and then do it.
- You are inside a spaceship, and you are looking out through a round window. What do you think you might see? Show me in Circle 9.
- Now think of Circle 6 as the sun, and think of Circle 11 as the earth. Shade in the part of Circle 11 — the earth — where you think it would be dark. Remember, the sunlight is coming from Circle 6.
- If you think of Circle 12 as a basketball, about how big would a baseball look? Draw a circle inside Circle 12 to show the size of the baseball. Now, how big would a grape look? Draw a circle inside the baseball circle to show the size of the grape. Now, how big would a fly look? Draw a little circle inside the grape circle to show the size of the fly.

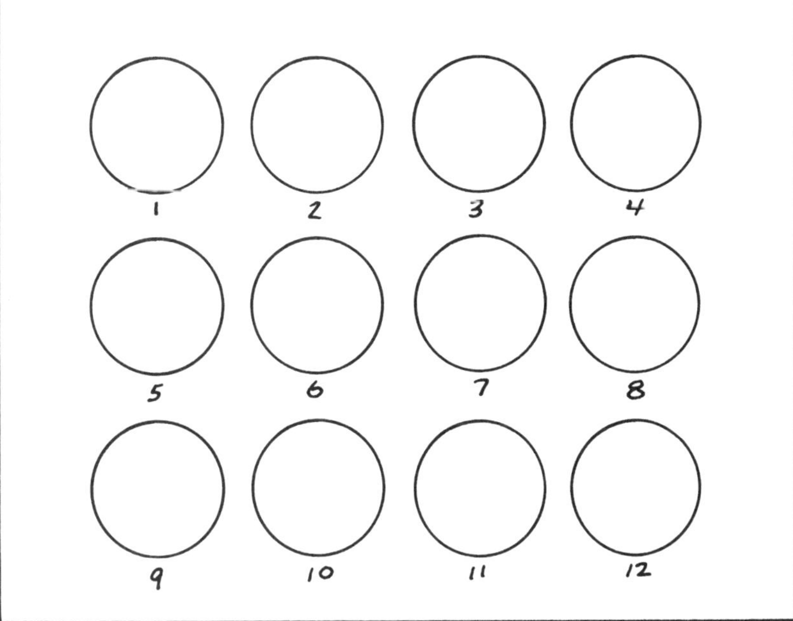

WORKSHEET SHOWN ABOVE. A SMALL JAR LID MAKES A GOOD PATTERN FOR THE CIRCLES.

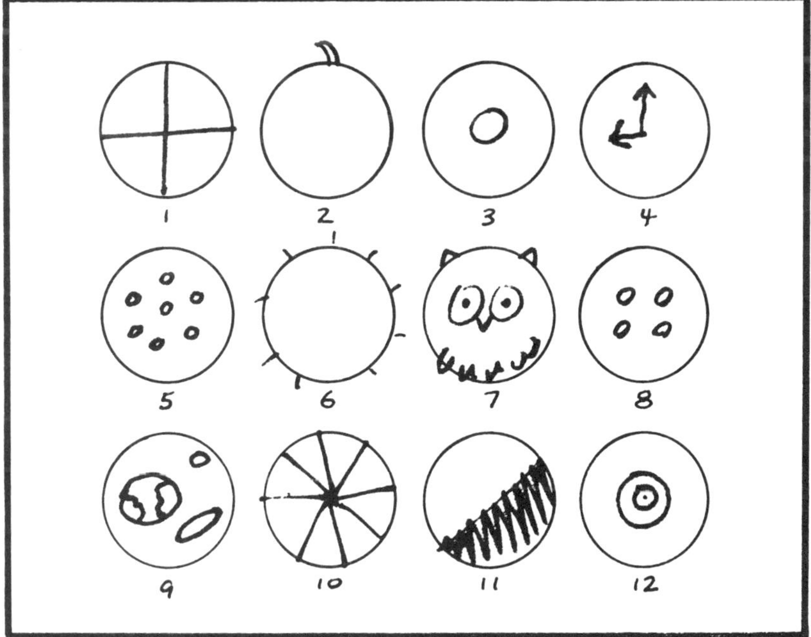

Matt Roberts, age 10

Use Your Head with Bread

About this activity...

This hands-on activity ought to hold their attention! Go out and buy the cheapest bread you can find — it makes fewer crumbs.

Materials needed...

A slice of bread for each student, plain paper, pencil.

Directions to students...

The name of our activity today is "Use Your Head With Bread." We'll be working with a real piece of bread, but you are not to do any nibbling until I say so, okay? I am now going to give you some directions which I want you to follow carefully. Are you ready?

- Put the piece of paper I have given you in the center of your desk with one of its short sides closest to you.
- Write your name at the bottom of the paper.
- Now, I'm going to give each of you a slice of bread. Put it in the middle of the piece of paper and then don't touch it until I tell you to do so. (Pass out bread.)
- To begin, I want you to use your pencil to trace all of the way around your piece of bread. Trace as closely as you can without actually touching the bread with the lead of your pencil.
- Now, pick up the bread. Take a small bite out of one of its sides. It's okay to eat the bite of bread.
- Take a larger bite out of another side.
- Take an even bigger bite out of another side.
- Put the bread back on the paper inside the shape you have drawn.
- Now, draw around the places where you made your bites. Don't let your pencil lead touch the bread.
- Pick up the bread again and bite a hole near the middle of the slice.
- Put the bread back on the outline and draw the hole you just made. Remember, don't touch the bread with your pencil lead.
- If you are hungry, you may now eat the rest of the bread. If you're not, bring it up to my desk and throw it away.

- Now, find a blank space on your paper and number 1-4. Answer these questions next to the numbers you just wrote.

Number 1. Did all the bites you made take away more than half of the bread? Write "yes" or "no" for your answer.

Number 2. About how many of the biggest bites would you have needed to eat the whole piece of bread?

Number 3. About how many of the smallest bites do you think you would have needed to eat the whole piece of bread? Take a guess!

Number 4. What do the bites you traced tell you about the shape of your mouth? Write your answer in a very short sentence.

THE FINISHED ASSIGNMENT WILL LOOK SOMETHING LIKE THIS.

A Macaroni Mystery

About this activity...

Questions about macaroni will lead students to the message, "Good to eat." Uncooked macaroni, with its tube-like characteristics, provides a thought-provoking prop as children grapple with the questions.

Materials needed...

One piece of elbow macaroni for each student, paper, pencil.

Directions to students...

Our activity today is called "Macaroni Mystery." Why a mystery? Because I will be giving you clues which will help you spell out a message which has something to do with macaroni. You'll need to listen and think carefully to solve the mystery. (Pass out macaroni.) Is everyone ready? Then, we'll get started.

- First, number 1-9 on the left-hand side of your paper.
- Now, look at one end of the macaroni. It forms a shape like one of the vowels. Which one? Put your answer next to Number 3. Your answer should just be one letter.
- Is a piece of macaroni more like a string, a tube or a pencil? Answer by putting an "s" for string, a "t" for tube or a "p" for pencil next to Number 9.
- Which of these words best describes a piece of macaroni — white, brown or tan? Answer by putting a "w" for white, a "b" for brown or a "t" for tan next to Number 5.
- To keep macaroni from spoiling, it must be kept wet, dry or frozen. Which is correct? Answer by putting a "w" for wet, a "d" for dry or an "f" for frozen next to Number 4.
- Is the piece of macaroni more like your head, your back or your elbow? Answer by putting an "h" for head, a "b" for back or an "e" for elbow next to Number 7.
- If you cook macaroni too long, it will probably get gooey, explode, or turn red. Answer with a "g" for gooey, an "e" for explode or an "r" for red next to Number 1.
- If you had three pieces of macaroni like the one you are using right now, which of these letters could you make most easily? An "o," a "b" or an "x?" Put your answer next to Number 6.

- Which of these might be able to hide inside of a piece of macaroni? A honeybee, an earthworm or an ant? Put an "h" for honeybee, an "e" for earthworm or an "a" for ant next to Number 8.
- Now, next to Number 2, write a letter of the alphabet that looks like your mouth before you take a big bite of macaroni. Did you put an "O?" Good for you!

If you followed directions and have thought carefully about your answers, you have spelled three words that have something to do with macaroni. What are they?

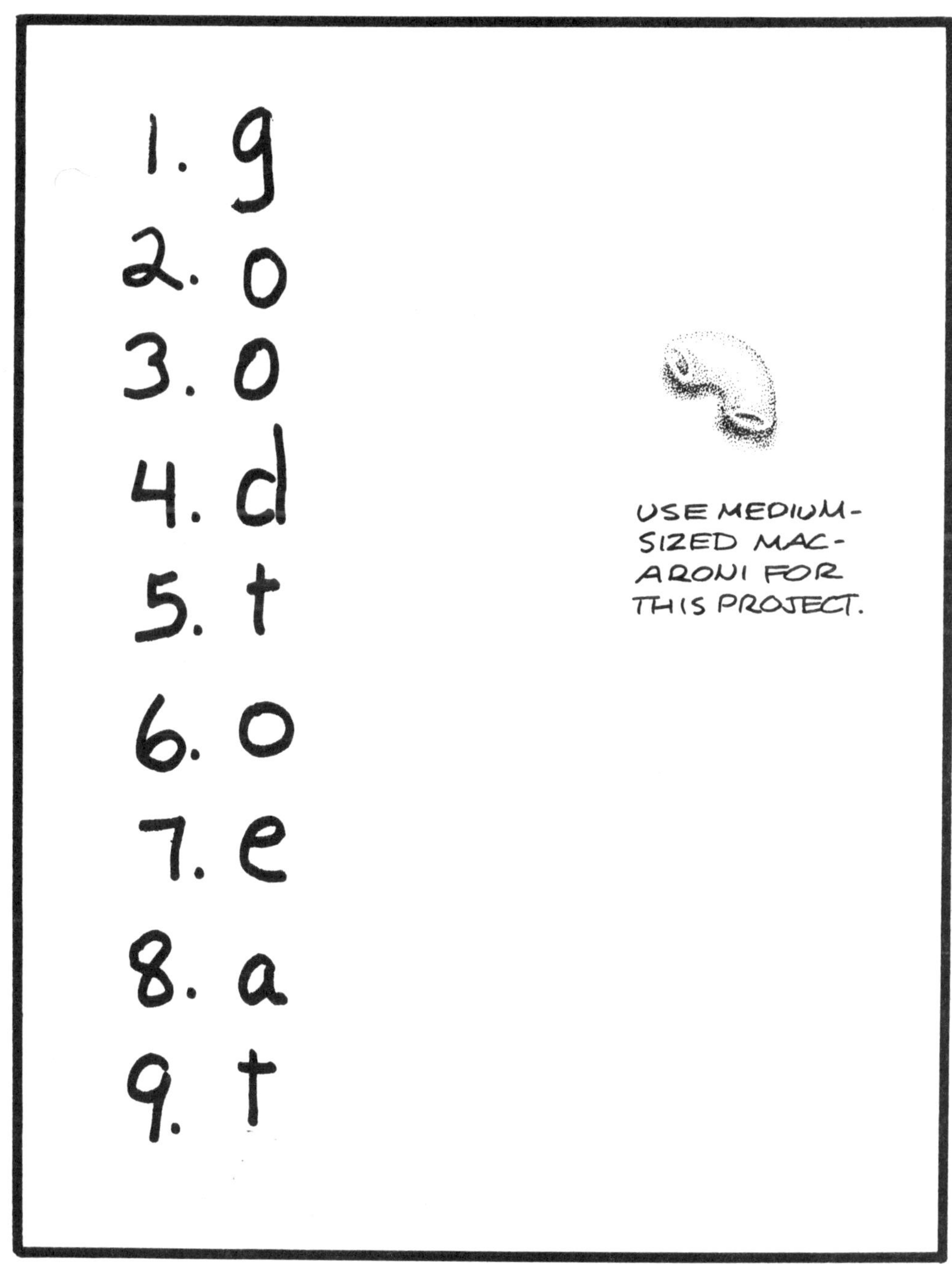

A Cracker Quiz

About this activity...

Children will be spelling out the word "crunchy" as they respond to questions about the properties of the cracker you have provided. Since they couldn't eat the macaroni, the cracker will be a welcome reward.

Materials needed...

One soda cracker for each student, paper, pencil.

Directions to students...

Today, we're going to take "A Cracker Quiz." It's not really a quiz. It is really another activity which asks you to listen, to follow directions, and to think. If you do this activity successfully, you will spell out a word that has something to do with crackers. (Pass out crackers.) You are *not* to eat your cracker until we have finished.

- To begin, number 1-7 on the left-hand side of your paper.
- Now, listen to these words: rough, smooth, fuzzy. Run your finger over the surface of the cracker and decide which word — rough, smooth or fuzzy — best describes what you feel. Then, next to Number 2, put an "r" for rough, an "s" for smooth or an "f" for fuzzy.
- Think about crackers and think about cookies. Which of these words describes something a cracker has and a cookie usually does not have? The words are: taste, holes and crumbs. Answer by putting a "t" for taste, an "h" for holes or a "c" for crumbs next to Number 6.
- Which of these three things would probably not eat a cracker unless it were very hungry — a mouse, a cat or a parrot? Answer by putting an "m" for mouse, a "c" for cat or a "p" for parrot next to Number 5.
- Now, look at the holes in the cracker. Does it look like they form a pattern of any kind? If your answer is "yes," put a "y" next to Number 7. If your answer is "no," put an "n" next to Number 7.
- Which could eat a cracker faster, a man or a mouse? Write the last letter in the word that is the best answer next to Number 4.
- Now, who knows how to spell the word "crumb?" Raise your hand if you do. (Take answers, discuss and then write the word "crumb" on the blackboard.) Okay, now answer this question: What is the only vowel in the word, "crumb?" Put your answer next to Number 3.
- Well, you have almost spelled a word that describes a cracker. Eat your cracker and write the letter which you think belongs next to Number 1.

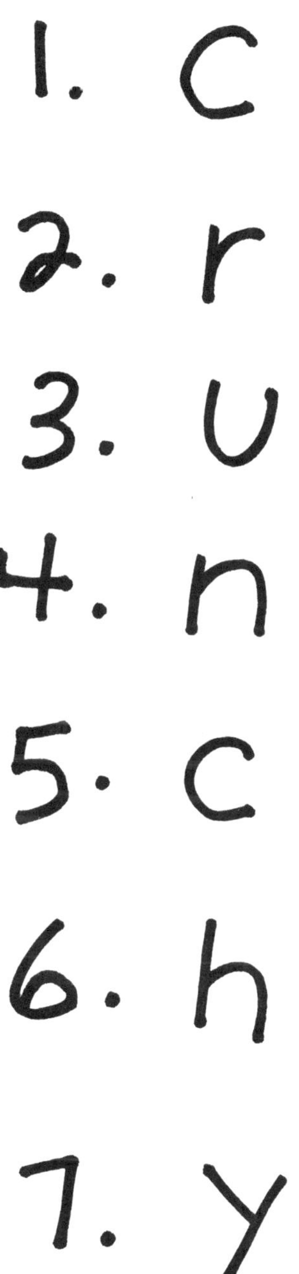

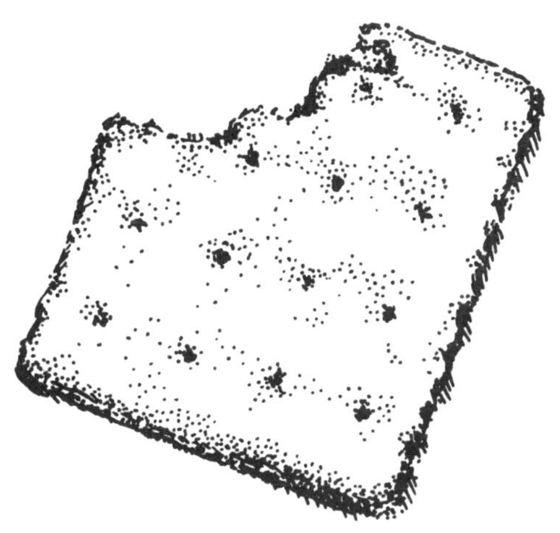

THIS ACTIVITY WILL NOT TAKE MUCH TIME, SO PLAN ACCORDINGLY.

Silly Letters

About this activity...

Children usually have to deal with letters in such a serious way that the liberties they are instructed to take here should provide a breath of fresh air. Keep the pacing crisp, and don't let children get too "precious" with the drawing.

Materials needed...

Worksheet (see illustration), pencil.

Directions to students...

Today, we're going to have some fun with letters. Use the paper I have given you. Use capital letters — not small letters — for your answers.

- In Box 8, draw an "R" which has fallen over.
- In Box 3, draw an "H" with feet.
- In Box 23, draw four "T's" in a row.
- In Box 19, draw a "P" you can hardly see.
- In Box 11, draw a "K" wearing ice skates.
- In Box 1, draw two "O's" laughing at a joke.
- In Box 9, draw a "V" and then turn it into an ice cream cone.
- In Box 6, make a bunch of scribbles and hide a "G" in them.
- In Box 20, make a "C" which is very fat.
- In Box 15, make a "U" which almost fills up the box.
- In Box 7, draw a "W" with an "M" on top of it.
- In Box 24, draw a "D" on its side and turn it into a little turtle.
- In Box 2, draw a backwards "S."
- In Box 5, make five "I's" that look like a fence.
- In Box 13, make three "H's" that look like a ladder.

- In Box 12, draw an "A" made by a very messy person.
- In Box 10, draw six little "O's" inside a big "O."
- In Box 21, draw a frontwards capital "B" and a backwards capital "B" to make a butterfly. This is hard, but try it.
- In Box 22, draw an "X" which touches each corner of the box.
- In Box 18, draw an "E" using dotted lines.
- In Box 14, make a very dark "H."
- In Box 17, put a "C" inside of an "O" and another "O" inside of the "C" you just drew.
- In Box 16, draw an "E" and then use your eraser to turn it into another letter.
- Oh, look, we're almost finished. In Box 4, draw a "Y" waving goodbye.

Jean Webster, age 9

BE SURE TO COMPARE RESULTS AT THE CONCLUSION OF THIS ACTIVITY. YOU'LL FIND LOTS OF VARIETY.

The Paper Wad Game

About this activity...

Paper wads? Well, at least there are no rubber bands associated with this game! Actually, the pace here is so rapid that there will be little time for traditional forms of paper-wad mischief.

Materials needed...

Plain paper (8½″ × 11″) and a strip of paper made by dividing a piece of 8½″ × 11″ paper into three vertical pieces.

Directions to students...

We are going to be playing "The Paper Wad Game" today, but first you must make your own game board and game pieces.

I have given each of you two pieces of paper. We'll start with the large piece first. Begin by folding the paper in half. Press down on the fold to make it good and sharp, and then fold it in half the other way.

Now, open up the paper and smooth it out. Go over the fold marks with your pencil so that it is easy to see the four boxes you have made. Next, place the paper so that one of the short sides is closest to you. Write the number "1" near the bottom of the top left-hand box. Write the number "2" near the bottom of the top right-hand box. Write the number "3" near the bottom of the lower left-hand box. Write the number "4" near the bottom of the lower right-hand box.

Now, let's make the game pieces — the paper wads. I'm sure you all know how to do that! First, tear the strip of paper into four parts. Try to make them about the same size. (pause) Now, crumple the four pieces into four little paper wads. By the way, the paper wads must stay on your desk or you don't get to play the game.

Now, we're ready to play. This is a game to see how well you listen and follow directions. You'll be showing me by moving the paper wads from box to box as I give you instructions.

Let's practice first. Put two of your paper wads in Box 3. (Don't use the other ones for now.) If I said "3 to 4," you would move one paper wad from Box 3 to Box 4. Okay, do that. Now, here's one rule: You never move more than one paper wad at a time, no matter how many wads happen to be in a particular box.

Let's practice again, starting with one paper wad in Box 3 and one in Box 4. The directions are: 4 to 2, 2 to 1. Now, where did your pieces end up? Yes, in Box 1 and 3.

Let's start. First, put one paper wad in each box. Here we go. Pay attention because I'm going fast.

- 4 to 2
- 3 to 1
- 1 to 2
- 2 to 4
- 1 to 2
- 4 to 2
- 2 to 1
- 2 to 3
- 1 to 4
- 2 to 1.

Where did the wads end up? Yes, one wad is in each box.

Next, let's start with all four paper wads in Box 2. This time, I'm going to go faster.

- 2 to 1
- 1 to 3
- 3 to 4
- 2 to 4
- 2 to 1
- 1 to 4
- 2 to 1
- 4 to 3
- 1 to 4
- 3 to 4

Where did the wads end up? Yes, they are all in Box 4.

Now, let's put two paper wads in Box 1 and two paper wads in Box 2. Here we go, and I'll be going very fast.

- 2 to 1
- 1 to 2
- 2 to 1
- 1 to 2
- 2 to 4
- 1 to 3
- 3 to 4
- 4 to 3
- 3 to 2

Where are the wads? Yes, there is one paper wad in Box 1, two paper wads in Box 2, and one paper wad in Box 4.

For this last game, I am going to say the directions faster than ever and there will be twice as many commands. Can you keep up with me? Start by putting all four wads in Box 1.

- 1 to 4
- 1 to 3
- 1 to 2
- 2 to 1
- 4 to 3
- 3 to 2
- 1 to 2
- 1 to 3
- 3 to 4
- 2 to 1
- 2 to 1
- 4 to 1
- 1 to 4
- 3 to 4
- 1 to 2
- 4 to 3.

How did you do? If you followed directions, each box should have a paper wad.

Puzzling Squares

About this activity...

The first part of the exercise does not tip off the fact that some interesting characters will be emerging. Most children seem to enjoy drawing strange faces, so this activity should be a natural.

Materials needed...

Worksheet (see illustration), pencil.

Directions to students...

Our activity today is called "Puzzling Squares." It is called that because at first you are not going to know what you are making.

- I have given you a piece of paper. Notice that there are five squares. Your first job is to number the squares 1-5, starting with Square 1 on the left. Put your number just beneath each square.

Are you ready? Then let's get started. Follow these directions carefully.

- Draw a small square in the middle of Square 5.
- Make a small bump that sticks out from the right-hand side of Square 2 about halfway up. Don't let it touch Square 3.
- Put a small triangle near the upper left-hand corner of Square 1. Put another small triangle near the upper right-hand corner of that same square.
- Make some dark scribbles all over the bottom half of Square 3.
- Put two circles of about the same size next to each other near the center of the top half of Square 3. Leave a little space between them.
- Put a large letter "C" somewhere near the middle of Square 2.
- Put a small square near the upper left-hand corner of Square 5. Put another small square near the upper right-hand corner of that same square.
- Put a small circle — but not too small — in the middle of Square 1.
- Draw a bow on top of Square 4.
- Put a little letter "c" inside the big letter "C" in Square 2.
- Draw a tall triangle on top of Square 1.
- Make some scribbles on top of Square 3.

- Draw a big letter "U" near the center of the bottom half of Square 4.
- Put a circle in the middle of each of the two top squares in Square 5.
- Put a small, upside-down "u" above the big "U" in Square 4. Put it somewhere near the center of the square.
- Put a small dot in the middle of each of the circles in Square 3.

Now, we're going to turn the squares into some faces, so listen carefully.

- Turn Square 1 into a sad clown with a droopy mouth, big ears and a fancy collar.
- Turn Square 2 into a side view of a smiling person wearing a baseball cap.
- Turn Square 3 into a man with a big nose who is wearing glasses.
- Turn Square 4 into a girl with big eyes, curly hair and freckles.
- Turn Square 5 into a robot with a large mouth, square ears and a skinny neck.
- Add any other details you wish.

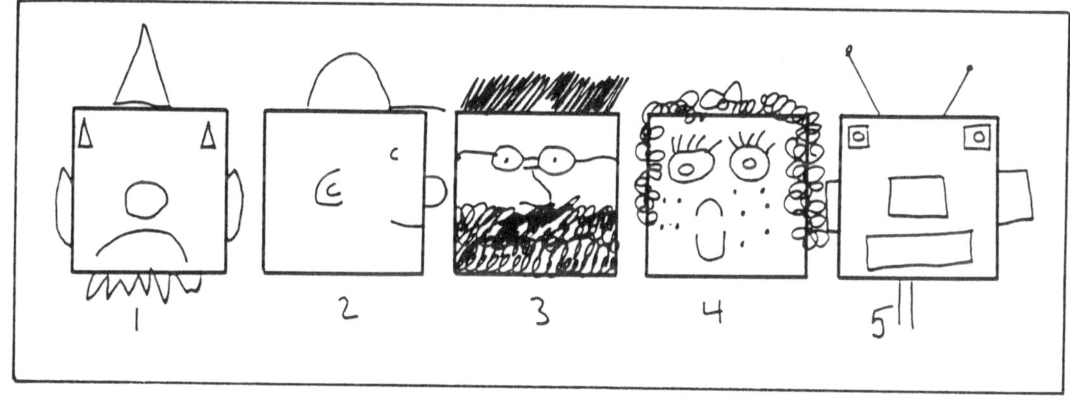

Aaron Van Scoy, age 11

BE SURE TO LEAVE SOME SPACE BETWEEN THE BOXES WHEN YOU MAKE THIS WORKSHEET.

Come to Dinner!

About this activity...

A formal table in this era of TV dinners? Why not?

Materials needed...

Worksheet (see illustration), pencil.

Directions to students...

It's time to eat — not really — but this assignment is called "Come to Dinner," so it has something to do with eating.

We are going to pretend we're getting a table ready for a big meal.

I have given you a sheet of paper with a big rectangle on it. That rectangle is going to be our table. We're going to pretend that we are looking at the table from above.

All right. Take out a pencil and let's begin.

Now, there are going to be four people eating at the table. There will be one person sitting at each end, and one person on each of the two sides.

- First, let's put four plates on the table. Show the plates by drawing four circles where you think they should go. Make the circles about this big (use your thumb and forefinger to indicate a circle about 1½" in diameter). Remember, you'll need one plate at each end and one plate on each side. Put the plates fairly close to the edge, so there will be room in the middle for some good, tasty food! You do not have to draw perfect circles. Just do your best.

- Next, we must add the napkins. Put the napkins to the left of each plate.

- Now, we have to do something about knives, forks and spoons. I want you to draw the knives first. Put them on the right-hand side of each plate. Remember, everything you are drawing should look like it is being seen from above.

- Now, we need four spoons. They should be a little shorter than the knives and should go just to the right of the knives.

- Next, let's give everyone a fork. The fork should go on the other side of the plate, right next to the plate and on top of the napkin.

- Now, let's give everyone a glass of milk. Let's still pretend we're looking at things from above. How would a glass look from above? Put it close to the point of the knife.

What should we have to eat? Since I'm the one fixing the dinner, I get to decide. I'll tell you this first. We're going to need one big platter and two big bowls for the food.

- Draw the platter and the bowls (as seen from above).
- In one of the bowls, draw a whole lot of peas.
- On the platter, draw enough fried chicken to please four hungry people. Think of drawing wings, drumsticks, other pieces.
- In the other bowl, we need a whole lot of mashed potatoes. How are you going to draw mashed potatoes as seen from above? You figure it out. Remember, these people are hungry!

Now, let's see. We have the plates, the silverware, the food. What else do we need? How about salt and pepper? Draw a salt shaker and a pepper shaker.

Okay. I think we're ready to eat. You may now add anything else you think we might need. How about a spoon for the mashed potatoes? What about some decoration on the plates? Should there be some flowers on the table? Butter on a dish? Rolls? Jam? You decide.

Sadie Boge, age 10

DRAW A LARGE RECTANGLE ON A SHEET OF 8½" x 11" PAPER FOR WORKSHEET.

Picture Surprises

About this activity...

This two-part activity starts with shapes and symbols which are then turned into pictures of familiar objects.

Materials needed...

Worksheet (see illustration), pencil.

Directions to students...

Our activity today is called "Picture Surprises." It is an activity in two parts. For the first part, you will need to listen and follow directions very carefully. For the second part, you will also have to listen, but you will need to do some thinking on your own. Let's begin by numbering the boxes 1-16, starting at the top left-hand box and going from left to right, row by row. Put the numbers beneath the boxes.

- In Box 1, draw a large plus sign. Leave some space between the plus sign and the edges of the box.
- In Box 2, draw three small circles side by side. Leave a little space between the circles.
- In Box 3, draw a tall, skinny "V." Start at the bottom of the box and leave some room at the top.
- In Box 4, draw a long, thin rectangle with its long sides going across, not up and down. Leave some room between the ends of the rectangle and the edges of the box.
- In Box 5, draw a simple shape that looks like a lake which you are looking at from above.
- In Box 6, draw two up-and-down lines next to each other . . . like an "11". Put them in the center of the box.
- In Box 7, make a large letter "J" in the middle of the box.
- In Box 8, draw two fairly small circles side by side. Put them in the middle of the box and leave a little space between them.
- In Box 9, draw a square which is about half as big as the box itself. Put it in the lower part of the box.
- In Box 10, make six small "1's" close together in a row near the right-hand side of the box.
- In Box 11, draw a shape like a person's eye . . . or like a canoe seen from above.
- In Box 12, draw a rectangle with its long sides about twice as long as its short sides.
- In Box 13, draw a large, upside-down capital letter "T." Leave room at the top and bottom of the box.
- In Box 14, draw three small letter "o's," one on top of another. Put them in the center of the box.
- In Box 15, draw a big letter "X" in the middle of the box.
- In Box 16, draw an upside-down letter "U." Put it in the top part of the box.

Now we're going to have some fun! I am going to give you some quick directions which you will use to turn all of the things we have just drawn into objects. Ready? Let's go!

- In Box 1, draw a square or rectangle to turn the plus sign into a window.
- In Box 2, use two more small circles to make a chain.
- In Box 3, use a capital letter "D" on its side to make an ice cream cone.
- In Box 4, add a letter "V" to make a shape like a pencil.
- In Box 5, add a circle to make a fried egg.
- In Box 6, use a letter "O" and a letter "U" to make a shape like a tin can.
- In Box 7, use one straight line and one curved line to make an umbrella.
- In Box 8, add any lines which you think are needed to make a pair of glasses.
- In Box 9, draw an upside-down letter "V" to make a shape like a house.
- In Box 10, use one straight line to make a toothbrush.
- In Box 11, use one triangle and one dot to make a fish.
- In Box 12, use two straight lines to make the back side of an envelope.
- In Box 13, use six straight lines of any length to make a sailboat.
- In Box 14, use one long rectangle and a straight line to make a stop-and-go light.
- In Box 15, use two letter "O's" to make a shape like a pair of scissors.
- In Box 16, use one straight line to make a hat.

CHILDREN MAY HAVE A BIT OF TROUBLE WITH QUESTIONS 6, 12 AND 13. GIVE SOME HINTS IF NECESSARY.

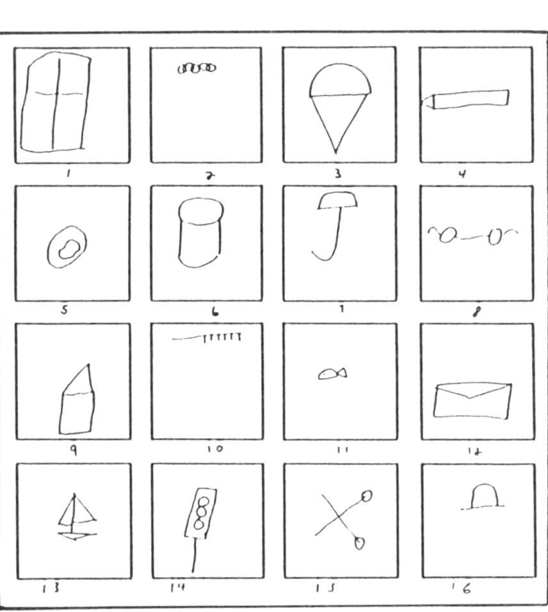

Brenna Woiwod, age 7

Our Room

About this activity...

Begin this activity with a walk around the room to make sure every child's "map" is oriented correctly — with the front of the room at the top.

Materials needed...

Worksheet (see illustration), pencil.

Directions to students...

I have just given you a map — at least, it's something like a map. Can anyone tell me what the map shows? Yes, it is a map of "Our Room."

To begin this activity, make sure the map is pointing in the direction you are facing. In other words, the front of the room should be shown on the top part of your paper.

- To begin, I want you to put a capital letter "T" to represent the place where I am standing right now.
- Next, find your own desk — where you are sitting now — on the paper and put your initials in the rectangle which stands for your desk.
- Now, make a rectangle showing where my desk should be.
- Inside the rectangle, put the capital letters "T-D" for "Teacher's Desk."

I'm afraid we have a problem! There is no way to go in or out of our room, is there?

- Give our room a door. Show the door by writing the letter "D" where the door should be.
- What about the windows? Show where the windows are by putting a "W" on the wall (or walls) where the windows are located.
- Let's also mark the place where the clock is found. Use the letter "C."

From where you are sitting right now, where do you live? Which direction?

- At the very top of your paper, outside the outline of our room, put a little arrow which points in the direction of the place where you live. Put an "H" for "Home" beside it.
- By the door, put another arrow pointing to the cafeteria (or any other school landmark). Put a "C" beside the arrow.

- Now, we're going to make a dotted line. I want you to show me, using a dotted line, where you would walk to get from your desk to the door.

- Who are a few of the people sitting closest to you? Put their initials in the rectangles that stand for their desks.

- Who do you think is sitting farthest away from you? Put that person's initials in the proper rectangle.

- Finally, think of five other important things in our room. (Blackboard, waste basket, closet, etc.) Show where they are located by writing the first letter in their names by the place where they are found.

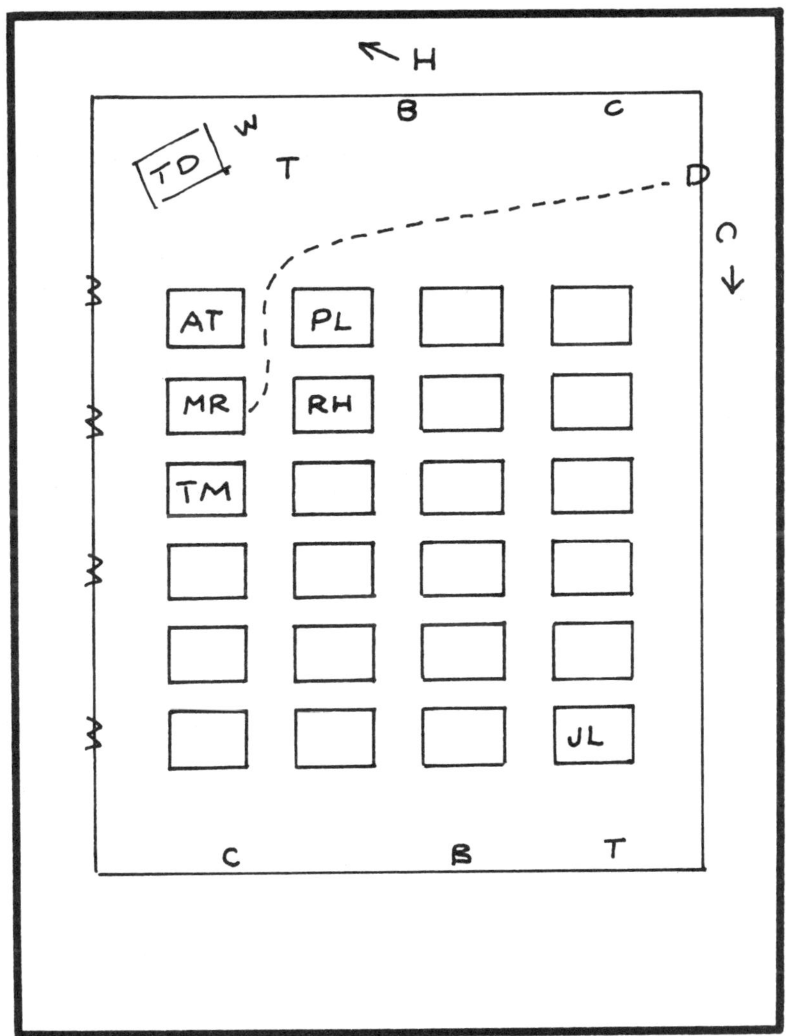

FURNISH A WORKSHEET WITH JUST THE OUTLINE OF YOUR ROOM AND STUDENTS' DESKS INDICATED. ALL OF THE OTHER DETAILS ARE TO BE ADDED BY CHILDREN.

Listen Up!

About this activity...

The last direction in this activity is obviously a joke — unless you have a circus contortionist in your midst. In any event, best to have a treat ready.

Materials needed...

Treat.

Directions to students...

Now we're going to play, "Listen Up," a game that is going to call for your best listening and direction-following skills.

The game goes like this: I'm going to ask you some questions which can be answered with a yes or a no. But you won't answer yes or no. You'll show me your answer by doing what I say.

There are two important rules. One — I will never repeat a question or the instructions. If you miss something I say, you'll just have to wait for the next question. Two — Don't do anything until I have finished talking and say the word, "Now!"

Let's start.

- Are you wearing shoes with laces today? If your answer is yes, put one hand on your head. If your answer is no, put both hands on your head. NOW.
- Are you wearing white socks? If your answer is yes, close your eyes. If your answer is no, touch your nose. NOW.
- Do you have any brothers or sisters? If your answer is yes, stand up. If your answer is no, spread both of your hands out on top of your desk. NOW.
- Do you have brown eyes? If your answer is yes, pat your head five times. If your answer is no, pat your stomach three times. NOW.
- Are there four or more letters in your whole first name (not your nickname)? If your answer is yes, hold one hand up in the air. If your answer is no, hold both hands up in the air. NOW.

Okay, the next several directions are going to get harder, because I'm going to give you two things to do, rather than just one.

- Do you like hamburgers better than fried eggs? If your answer is yes, pretend you're eating a hamburger and then pretend you're sipping from a straw. If your answer is no, pretend you're eating a fried egg with a fork and then pretend you're drinking a glass of milk. NOW.

2's — Tap on your desk three times.

3's — Tap on your desk one more time than the 2's did.

1's — Tap on your desk one more time than the 3's did.

Now that I have you tapping, we're going to get down to some really serious desk-tapping. Here's how it works. I will tap a pattern of knocks on my desk, and then call a number. If your number is called, you tap the same pattern back to me.

Tap — tap — pause — tap . . . 3's.

Tap — pause — tap — tap . . . 1's.

Tap — tap — tap — tap — pause — tap . . . 2's.

Tap — pause — tap — tap — pause — tap . . . 1's and 3's.

(Continue on, using your own tapping patterns. Always establish the pattern before calling the group number or numbers.)

A Paper Clip Picture

About this activity...

Here's a hands-on activity guaranteed to produce a cute rabbit and some sunshine! Make sure children understand they don't have to trace around the paper clip perfectly.

Materials needed...

Worksheet (see illustration), two standard-sized paper clips for each student, pencil.

Directions to students...

Our activity today is called "A Paper Clip Picture." I have given each of you two paper clips, which you will be using in different ways to do the things I ask you to do. Are you ready?

- First, place your paper so that one of its short sides is nearest to you.
- Now, number the squares 1-8, starting at the top left-hand square and going from left to right, row by row. Put your numbers in the lower left-hand corner of each square.

Now we come to the fun part... the picture.

- In Square 4, make a circle about as big around as a quarter. Make it touch the bottom edge of the square, and put it near the middle of the line.
- Place one of your paper clips with its long side touching the bottom edge of Square 3. Use your pencil to trace around the outside of the paper clip to make an outline. It's hard to hold the paper clip and trace at the same time, but do your best. Your outline doesn't have to be perfect. Just give us the idea.

Well, our picture doesn't look like much yet, does it? But it will soon!

- I want you to think of the circle you just drew in Square 4 as the head of a rabbit. Put two paper clips where you think the ears should be and then draw around them.
- Now, give your rabbit two eyes, a nose, a mouth and some whiskers.
- The rabbit you just drew really does have a body. You just can't see it, because the rabbit is peeking over the top of a fence. Use all of Squares 5 and 6 to make the fence. Give it boards that go up and down.
- Let's pretend that the fence you just drew doesn't reach all of the way to the ground and that you can see the rabbit's feet beneath the bottom of the boards. Draw around two paper clips to make the feet.

- The rabbit looks a little lonesome, doesn't it? Let's give it a friend. Turn the outline of the paper clip you drew in Square 3 into a friendly caterpillar.
- Let's pretend it's a sunny day. Draw the sun in Square 1. Make it about as big around as the length of a paper clip.
- Now, let's put a flower down in Square 7. Can you think of a way to draw around the same paper clip several times to make the flower's petals? Try it now. You may also give the flower a stem and some leaves if you wish.
- Square 2 is still empty, isn't it? You *must* draw something in Square 2, but what you draw is up to you. There is just one rule. Whatever you draw must include the outline of at least one paper clip.

MAKE BOXES ABOUT 2½" SQUARE TO ACCOMMODATE THE SIZE OF PAPER CLIPS.

Joey Slabaugh, age 10

Get There

About this activity...

Children will be weaving their way through an obstacle course which grows in complexity as the activity progresses. The adventure of "getting there" should provide a lot of fun.

Materials needed...

Worksheet (see illustration), pencil.

Directions to students...

Today, we are going to do some traveling on paper. The activity is called, "Get There!" I have given you a paper with 16 numbered circles. Let's think of the circles as 16 places you'll be visiting.

When I say to go from one place to another, you will be drawing a line between any edge of one circle to any edge of another circle. But there are two rules: None of your lines can touch other circles or go through other circles, and none of your lines can touch other lines.

I'll also give you these hints: It is best to keep your lines in the middle of the rows and not to make them too close to other lines if you can help it. This is because you'll be making a lot of lines and you'll need room to draw them. Also, try to take the shortest path between circles at the beginning of the activity. The lines you draw can go anywhere on the paper...but remember, you cannot cross lines or touch other circles. Are you ready?

Draw a line from:

- 1 to 7.
- 8 to 11.
- 14 to 6.
- 4 to 16.
- 15 to 3.
- 10 to 12.
- 9 to 2.
- 5 to 13.

That wasn't too hard, was it? But now your trips are going to get more difficult!

Draw a line from:

- 2 to 8.
- 13 to 16.
- 9 to 6.
- 5 to 10.
- 12 to 1.
- 11 to 4.

Now, there is one trip left, and it's going to be a hard one. Can you get from 3 to 13? Try it!

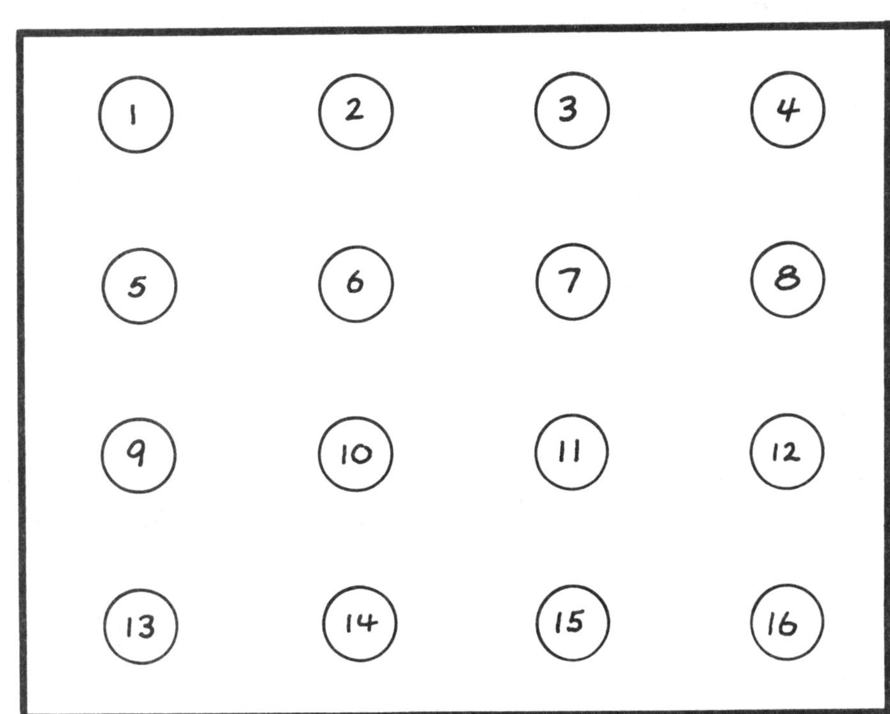

PROVIDE WORKSHEET WITH 16 NUMBERED CIRCLES. USE SAME WORKSHEET FOR ALL THREE OF THE "GET THERE" ACTIVITIES.

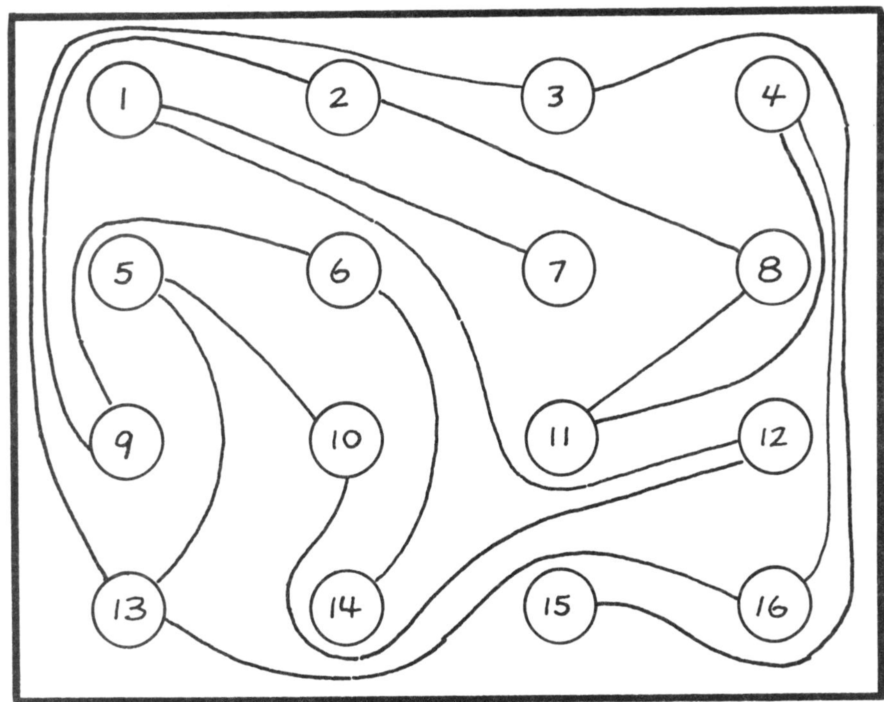

A POSSIBLE "SOLUTION."

Get There (2)

About this activity...

Students are given some freedom to choose their own routes, but they must depart from and arrive at the places you specify. The coloring aspect of the activity makes them accountable.

Materials needed...

Worksheet (see illustration on page 43), pencil, crayons.

Directions to students...

We're going to do another "Get There!" activity today, but this trip will be slightly different. We'll still be going from circle to circle, but part of the time I will be telling you how to get there.

This time, it is okay to cross lines, unless you are told not to do so. But you are never to make a line through a circle. To do this activity well, you must listen very carefully.

Before we begin, get out a pencil, a red crayon, a blue crayon and a yellow crayon. Set the crayons aside. You'll need just your pencil at first.

All right, let's start.

- First, with your pencil, draw a line between 9 and 11.
- Draw a line between 6 and 14, crossing one line on the way.
- Draw a line between 2 and 4 which goes below 3.
- Draw a line between 1 and 8 which goes above 2, 3 and 4.
- Draw a line between 12 and 5 which goes between 7 and 11 and above 6.
- Draw a line between 16 and 3. The line you draw must cross two other lines on the way.
- Without crossing any lines, draw a line which goes from 1, down and around 13, and back to 5.
- Draw a line between 7 and 8. Remember, if you cross a line or lines, that's okay unless I say not to do so.
- Draw a line from 15 to 4, and make the line you draw cross through four lines.
- Draw a line from 16 to 11 without crossing any other lines.
- Starting at 9, go under 14, above 15, and end up at 16. You may cross as many lines as you wish.

- Now, make a trip from 1 to 11, crossing as few lines as possible.
- Connect 16 to 15 by crossing three lines.

For this last part, you'll need your crayons.

- First, if you followed directions correctly, you should be able to find two circles which have no lines coming from them. Color them yellow.
- You should have two circles with three lines coming from them. Color them blue.
- Finally, you should have just one circle with four lines coming from it. Color it red.

Now, no matter how you drew your lines, everyone should have circles of the same color in the same place. Let's see how you did!

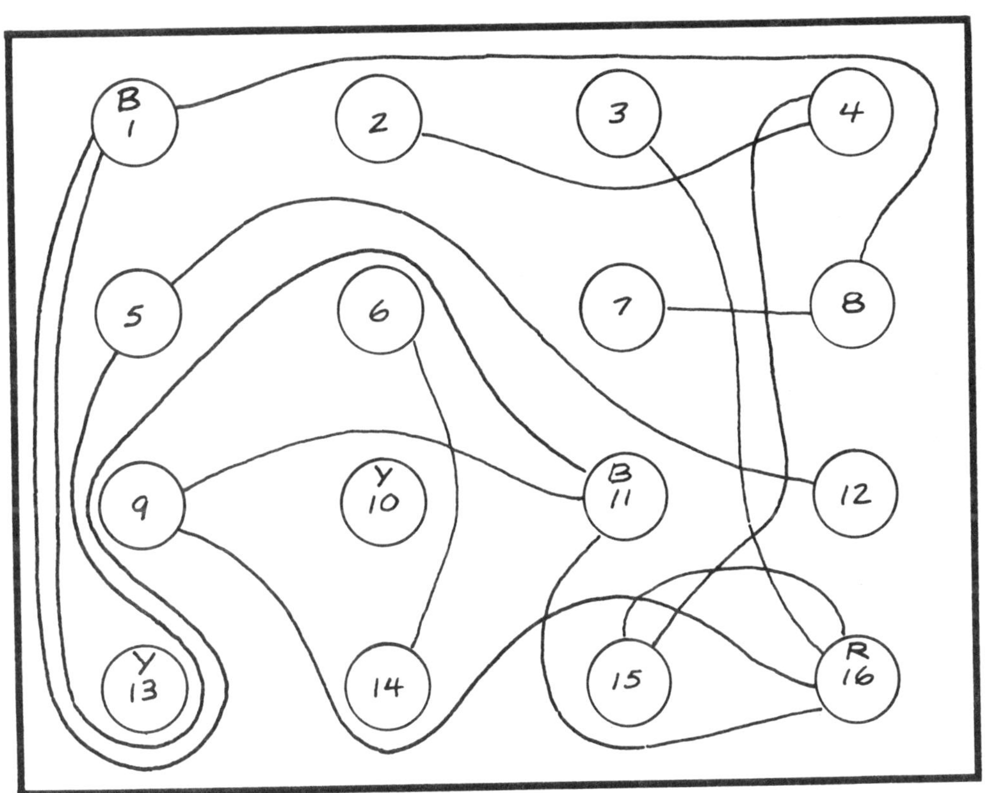

A COMPLETED "GET THERE" ACTIVITY. RED, BLUE AND YELLOW INDICATED BY R-B-Y.

Get There (3)

About this activity...

Here is another chance for children to have great fun while following directions. The next-to-the-last journey is actually quite difficult (7-12, four lines).

Materials needed...

Worksheet (see illustration on page 43), pencil, crayons.

Directions to students...

How would you like to go on another traveling adventure? This "Get There!" activity will be a lot like the other two we have done before. We'll still be going from circle to circle, and some of the time I will be telling you what to do to get there.

It is okay to cross lines unless I tell you not to do so, but you are never to make a line through a circle.

Before we begin, get out a pencil, a red crayon and a blue crayon. Set the crayons aside. You will need just your pencil at first.

Okay, let's start our journey.

- First, with your pencil, draw a line from 1 which goes to the left of 5, 9 and 13 and then takes the shortest path to 4.
- Starting at 6, go around 9 and back to 10.
- Go from 2 to 15 by crossing three lines.
- Start at 3 and go to 11 without crossing any lines.
- Go from 6 to 11 by crossing just one line.
- Start at 14, go above 12, and end up at 16.
- From 1, go around 5, and end up at 2 without crossing any lines.
- Go from 6 to 16 without crossing any lines.
- Go from 7 to 12 by crossing any four lines.
- From 13, try to go to 2 without crossing any lines.

Now, let's see how well you listened.

- If you followed directions correctly, there should be three circles which have no lines coming out from them. Color them blue.

- There should be two circles which have three lines coming out from them. Color them red.

Each of you may have taken different paths to get to the circles I named, but all of you should have circles of the same color in the same places. Let's see how you did.

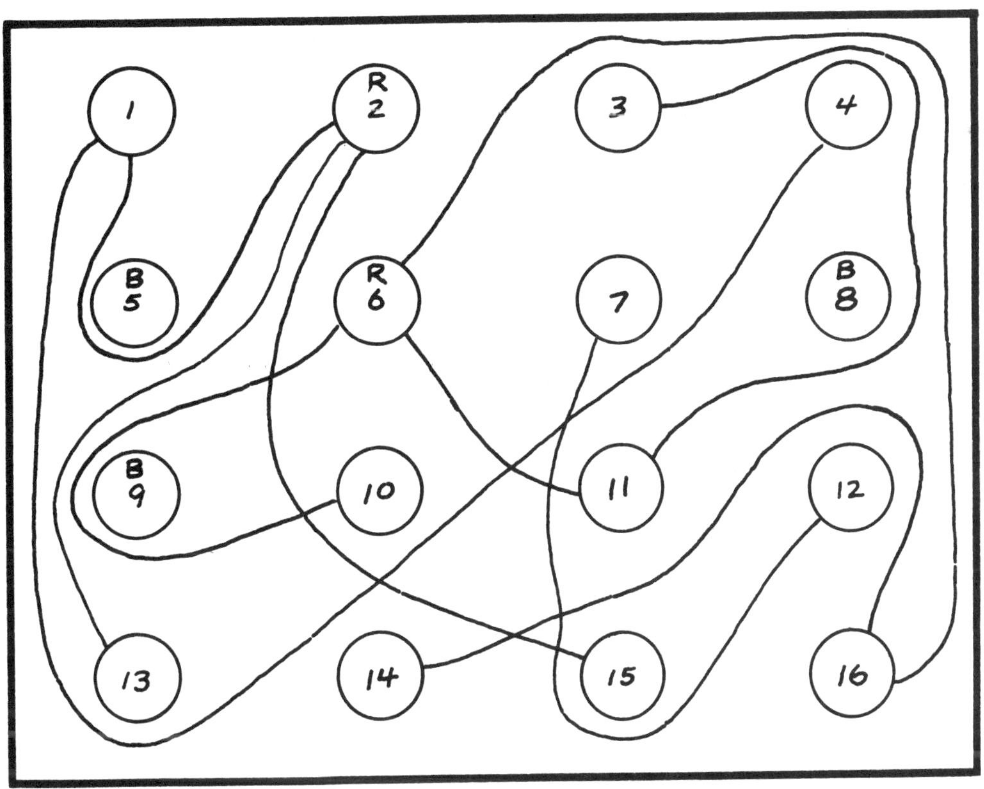

A COMPLETED ACTIVITY. BLUE AND RED ARE INDICATED BY B-R.

A Letter Chase

About this activity...

Everyone likes a mystery, and the message here should remain mysterious until the very end — or almost until the very end. The colored blocks simply provide "stops" between the words in crossword puzzle fashion.

Materials needed...

Worksheet (see illustration), pencil, crayons.

Directions to students...

Today, we're going to play a game called "A Letter Chase." You are going to write a sentence by putting letters in the numbered boxes you see on the sheet of paper I have given you.

First, let's do some coloring. Please take out your crayons and follow these directions.

- Color Box 2 red. (pause) Color Box 9 blue. (pause) Use a green crayon to color Box 10. (pause) Color Box 30 brown. (pause) Find Box 25 and color it orange.

Now, put away your crayons. You will need just a pencil for the rest of this activity. From now on, each answer you give will be in the form of a letter, which you are to put in the correct box. I will go fairly quickly, so listen carefully.

- Look at Box 2. What is the middle letter in the name of the color in Box 2? Put that letter in Box 14.
- What is the first letter in the word, "letter?" Put it in Box 28.
- There is a three-letter word which means the opposite of "dry." Put the first letter in that word in Box 26.
- Put the same letter you put in Box 28 in Box 5.
- If you asked for ice cream and candy for breakfast, what two-letter word would an adult probably say to you? Put the first letter of that word in Box 19.
- Which letter of the alphabet looks most like a ball? Put that letter in Box 18.
- An insect that buzzes and makes honey has a name which includes two letters that are the same. Put one of those two letters in Box 22.
- What is the letter that comes after the letter "K" in the alphabet? Put that letter in Box 6.
- Now, go to Box 50. (Wait for reaction.) Oops! There is no Box 50, is there? Well, let's do Box 7. What is the first letter in the word, "oops?" Put it in Box 7.
- Hello! I am (your name). Who are YOU? What's the first letter in the last word I just said? Put it in Box 24.

- Now, we're looking for a one-letter word. What is the one-letter word you would use when talking about yourself? Put it in Box 12.
- Find the box you colored green. If you spelled out the number of the green box, what is the first letter you would use? Put it in Box 16.
- You might see one of these sitting on a lily pad, and you might hear it croak. It is the same color as the color you put in Box 10. What is the first letter in its name? Put that letter in Box 3.
- Do you remember that letter that looks like a ball? Here it comes again! Put that letter in Box 4.

Can you figure out what words we are spelling yet? If you can, don't say them out loud!

- What is the first letter in the five-letter word that describes the kind of day it is when you see a lot of people with umbrellas? Put it in Box 23.
- What is the last letter in the word that means the opposite of "no?" The *last* letter. Put it in Box 20.
- What letter did you put in Box 28? Put that same letter in Box 29.
- This animal likes to chase cats. What is it called? Put the first letter of its name in Box 11.
- What is the middle letter in the name of a bird that flies at night and says, "Hoot?" Put that letter — the middle letter — in Box 8.
- What letter am I making now? (Make a "V" sign with your fingers.) Put it in Box 21.
- What is the first letter in the name of an animal that has a trunk? Put it in Box 27.
- Remember that question about dogs chasing things? What is the first letter in the name of the thing dogs like to chase? Put it in Box 15.
- You spelled an important word in Box 12. Spell it again in Boxes 1 and 17.
- Ah! Finally! One more box! Which letter should we put in Box 13? (Discuss. The letter, of course, is "R.")

i 1	RED 2	f 3	o 4	l 5	l 6	o 7	w 8	BLUE 9	GREEN 10
d 11	i 12	r 13	e 14	c 15	t 16	i 17	o 18	n 19	s 20
v 21	e 22	r 23	y 24	ORANGE 25	w 26	e 27	l 28	l 29	BROWN 30

USE HALF A PIECE OF 8½"x11" PAPER FOR THIS.

A Letter Chase (2)

About this activity...

You'll get some moans and groans once students eliminate the false "A" clues and get the message.

Materials needed...

Worksheet (see illustration), pencil.

Directions to students...

Are you ready for another "Letter Chase" game? I'm not sure you're going to agree with what the message has to say, but we'll see.

Let's go over the rules. Remember, I will be giving you clues which you will use to figure out which letters go in which boxes. By the time you are finished, you will have spelled out a sentence. All you will need today is a pencil and the piece of paper I have given you. Are you all set? Let's go!

- What is the first letter in the name of something that shines in the sky during the day? Put that letter in Box 17.
- You need a "b," a "k," and two of these letters in the middle to spell the word "book." Put one of those middle letters in Box 15.
- What sound does a cow make? Put the first letter of the word we use to describe that sound in Box 24.
- Which letter of the alphabet looks most like what a chicken lays? Put it in Box 27.
- Here's an easy one. Put the first letter of the alphabet in Boxes 2 and 10.
- Oops! The chicken has done it again! It has laid another of those things that look like a letter. Put the letter in Box 9.
- When you wash your hands at a sink, you often see two letters. One is a "C." What is the other letter? Put it in Box 22.
- Remember those round things the chicken laid? It has happened again in Boxes 19 and 23.
- Put the fifth letter of the alphabet in Box 6.
- Which letter of the alphabet comes between "C" and "E?" Put that letter in Box 11.
- What is the first letter in the name of the meal you eat at school in the middle of the day? Put it in Box 14.
- One letter of the alphabet looks like a letter "M" which has been turned upside-down. Which one is it? Put it in Box 26.
- Oh, my! I hear that chicken again! This time it has hopped into Box 4 and laid another of those shapes that look like an alphabet letter.

- Think of a little mound of dirt with lots of insects crawling around. Sometimes these insects come to picnics. What is the first letter in their name? Put it in Box 21.
- What is the first letter in the word that means the opposite of "true?" Put it in Box 20.
- Speaking of opposites, what is the first letter in the word that is the opposite of "short?" Put it in Box 8.
- What is the first letter in the name of the room where you find a stove and refrigerator? Put it in Box 29.
- You see a lot of red hearts on this special day. What is the first letter in the name of this day? Put it in Box 5.
- What is the first letter in the three-letter word for something water becomes when it freezes? Put that letter in Box 1.
- If I were saying the alphabet over and over, which letter would I say each time after I said the letter "Z?" Put that letter in Boxes 7, 13, 18 and 30.
- Cackle, cackle! Put another of those round things in Box 12.
- The U.S. flag is blue, white and another color which starts with this letter. Put it in Box 28.
- I see these every time you give me a big smile. They stay nice and white if you brush them. Put the first letter in their name in Box 16.
- If you spelled the word "elbow" the way it sounds, you would probably use this letter first. Put it in Box 3.
- What is it that chickens lay? They lay something that "looks" like a letter, but of course the thing they lay has a name. What is the first letter in that name? Put it in Box 25.

Now, we have spelled a message. But there seems to be something wrong. There are some letters which don't belong. Actually, there is just *one* letter — one letter repeated several times — that is getting in the way of the message. Can you figure out which letter it is? When you do, cross it out every time you find it.

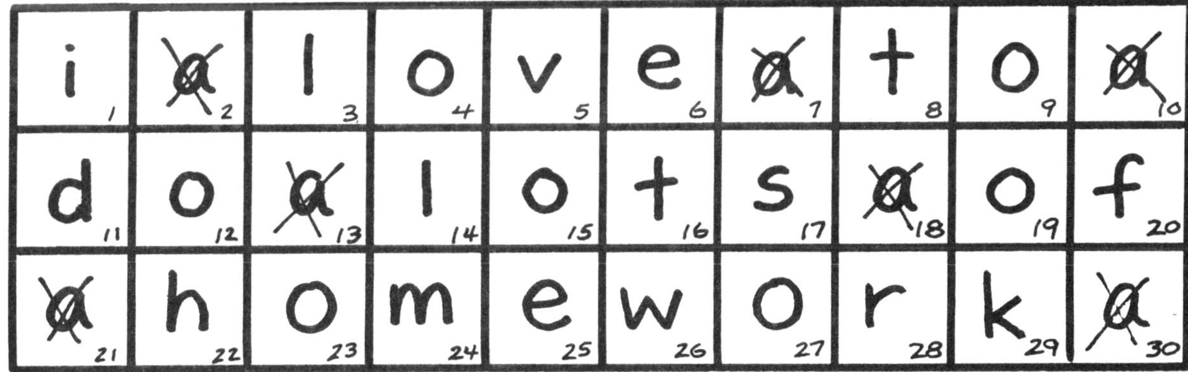

THIS WORKSHEET IS THE SAME AS THAT USED FOR THE FIRST "LETTER CHASE" ACTIVITY.

Lucky Dots

About this activity...

The element of chance at work in the following series of "Lucky Dots" and "Lucky Dots and Lines" activities guarantees high interest.

Materials needed...

Plain paper, pencil, crayons, ruler.

Directions to students...

Today, we're going to play a game called "Lucky Dots." How you do will depend on how lucky you are, but you must follow directions carefully.

I have given you two pieces of paper. You will also need a pencil, your crayons and a ruler.

First, use your pencil to number 1-8 on one of your pieces of paper, starting with number one and going down to number eight. Set that paper aside when you are finished.

Now, on the sheet of blank paper, I want you to use your pencil to draw 15 little circles. Make them about the size of a pea, and spread them out all across the paper.

Next, make one big circle — about the size of your thumbnail — anywhere on your paper.

Now, it's time to do some folding. First, I want you to fold the paper — the one with the circles — in half. Press down on the fold to make it good and sharp. Leave your paper folded, and then fold it in half in the other direction. Fold it one more time... and then once more. Make sure you crease the folds.

Open up the paper and smooth it out. You should see 16 small boxes made by the fold marks.

Next, we need to do some coloring. First, I want you to color any five of the little circles red. (pause) Now, color any five of the little circles blue. (pause) Color the last five little circles green. (pause) Finally, color the big circle orange.

Okay, now it's time to play the game. You will be using the paper you numbered 1-8 to keep track of your score.

- Number 1. If you have any boxes with no dots in them, give yourself one point for each empty box. If not, give yourself a zero.

- Number 2. If each of your red dots is in a separate box, give yourself two points.

- Number 3. Give yourself one point for each dot that is touching a fold line. (Including the big orange dot.)

- Number 4. If you have a total of five or more dots all the way inside the four corner boxes, give yourself one point.

- Number 5. Find the two green dots that are the farthest apart. Use your ruler to draw a straight line between them. It's okay if your line passes through another dot. (pause) Now, count the number of boxes your straight line passes through. Give yourself one point for each box your line touches.

- Number 6. If you have any boxes with a blue dot and a red dot all the way inside the same box, give yourself two points for each box in which that happens.

- Number 7. If you have two dots of any color all the way inside any one box, give yourself one point for each box in which that happens.

- Number 8. Now for the big dot. Where is it? If your big dot is all the way inside a box — not touching any fold line — give yourself three points.

Now, who has the most points? Add up your score and let's see how you did.

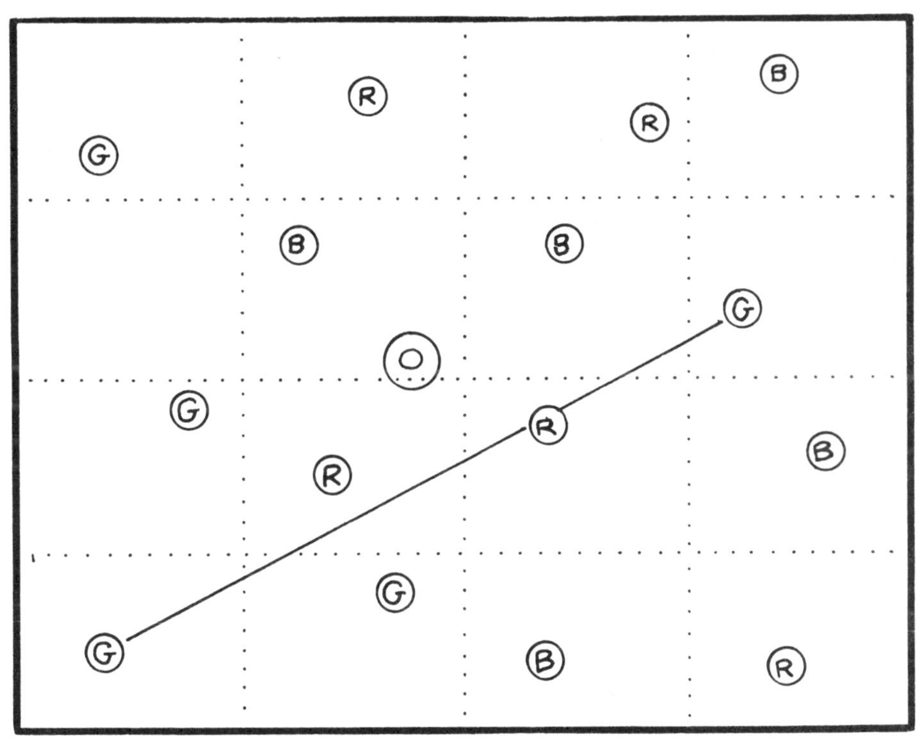

FOLD MARKS INDICATED BY DOTTED LINES. COLORS RED, BLUE, GREEN AND ORANGE ARE REPRESENTED BY R-B-G-O. THE SCORE FOR THIS VERSION WOULD BE 10.

Lucky Dots (2)

About this activity...

Just when they thought they had the system figured out, someone changed the rules!

Materials needed...

Plain paper, pencil, crayons, ruler.

Directions to students...

Are you ready to play another "Lucky Dots" game?

I have given you two pieces of paper. You will also need a pencil, your crayons and a ruler.

First, use your pencil to number 1-8 on one of your pieces of paper, starting with number one and going down to number eight. Set that paper aside when you are finished.

Now, on the blank sheet of paper, use your pencil to draw 15 little circles. Make them about the size of a pea, and spread them out all across the paper. (pause) Next, make three bigger circles — about the size of your thumbnail — anywhere on your paper.

It's time now to do some folding. First, I want you to fold the paper — the one with the circles — in half. Press down on the fold to make it good and sharp. Leave your paper folded, and then fold it in half in the other direction. Fold it one more time... and then once more. Make sure you crease the folds.

Open up your paper and spread it out. You should see 16 small boxes made by the fold marks.

Now, place the piece of paper with one of its long sides closest to you and number the boxes 1-16, starting at the top left-hand box and going from left to right, row by row.

Next, we need to do some coloring. First, I want you to color any five of the little circles red. (pause) Now, color any five of the little circles blue. (pause) Color the last five little circles green. (pause) Finally, color the three big circles brown.

Okay, let's start the game. Remember, use the paper numbered 1-8 to keep track of your score.

- Number 1. Look at boxes one, five and nine. Give yourself one point for every dot that is completely inside those boxes.
- Number 2. How many of your brown dots are touching any fold line? Give yourself one point for every brown dot that is touching a fold.
- Number 3. Look at the blue dots. Use your pencil and ruler to draw the biggest triangle you can, using three of the blue dots for the three corners of the triangle. (pause) Count the number of boxes the lines go through. Give yourself one point for every box the lines touch.

- Number 4. Do any of your boxes contain two or more dots of the same color? If any of your boxes have two or more dots of the same color all the way inside the box, give yourself two points for each of those boxes. (It doesn't matter if there are other colors in the box.)

- Number 5. Now, find the two green dots that are closest together and use your ruler to draw a straight line between them. (pause) Do the same thing with the two red dots that are closest together. (pause) If the line between the two green dots is shorter than the line between the two red dots, give yourself one point. If it is longer, give yourself a zero.

- Number 6. If you have a red dot all the way inside any odd-numbered box (1-3-5, etc.), give yourself a point for each box in which that happens.

- Number 7. If you have a green dot all the way inside any even-numbered box (2-4-6, etc.), give yourself a point for each box in which that happens.

- Number 8. If you can draw a straight line to connect any two of the brown dots without running into a line you have already drawn, do it now and give yourself three points.

Now, let's figure out who has the most points. Add up your score to see how you did.

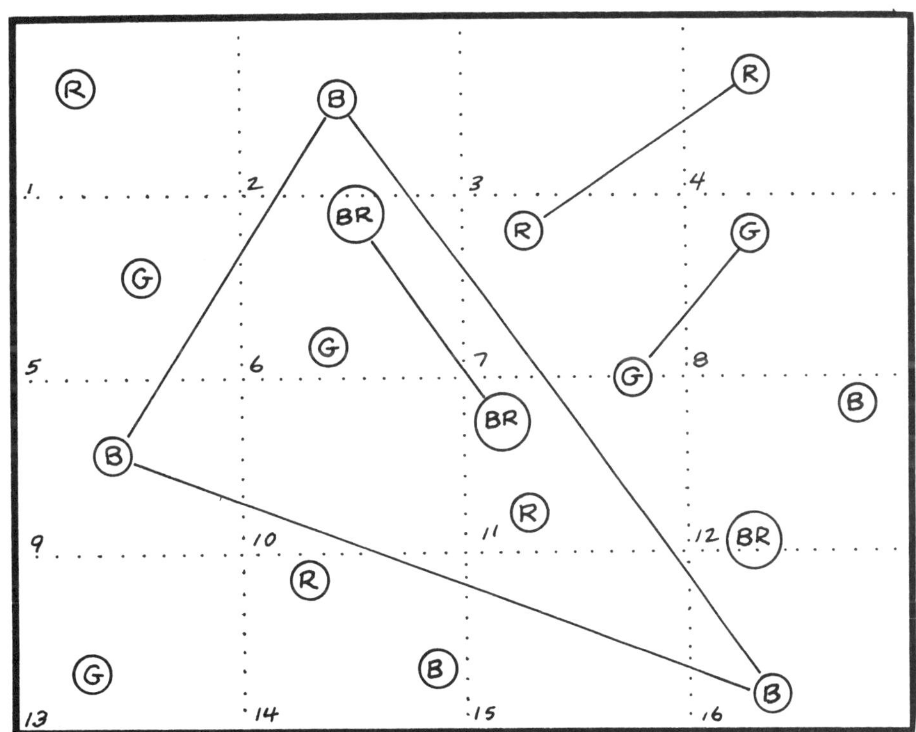

Lucky Dots and Lines

About this activity...

The addition of lines provides a new twist. At this point the level of competition should be rising. The number of "creative" interpretations of the rules will probably also be on the rise as children seek to maximize scores.

Materials needed...

Plain paper, pencil, crayons, ruler.

Directions to students...

Today, we are going to play a game called "Lucky Dots and Lines."

The rules of the game will be about the same as they were in the "Lucky Dots" games we played.

I have given you two pieces of paper. You will also need a pencil, your crayons and a ruler.

First, use your pencil to number 1-8 on one of your pieces of paper, starting with number one and going down to number eight. Set that paper aside when you are finished.

Now, on the blank sheet of paper, use your pencil to draw 16 little circles. Make them about the size of a pea, and spread them out all across the paper. (pause) Next, make two bigger circles — about the size of your thumbnail — anywhere on your paper.

It's time now to do some folding. First, I want you to fold the paper — the one with the circles — in half. Press down on the fold to make it good and sharp. Leave your paper folded, and then fold it in half in the other direction. Fold it one more time... and then once more. Make sure you crease the folds.

Open up your paper and spread it out. You should see 16 small boxes made by the fold marks.

Now, place the piece of paper with one of its long sides closest to you and number the boxes 1-16, starting at the top left-hand box and going from left to right, row by row.

Next, we need to do some coloring. First, I want you to color any six of the little circles green. (pause) Now, use a red crayon to make a small circle around any two of the green dots. (pause) Next, color any two of the little circles purple. (pause) Now, color the rest of the little circles black. (pause) Color one of the big circles brown. (pause) Finally, color the other big circle orange.

Okay, let's start the game. Remember, use the paper numbered 1-8 to keep track of your score.

- Number 1. Use your pencil and ruler to draw a straight line that goes through both of the purple dots and out to both edges of the paper. (pause) If the line you drew touches any dots besides the purple dots, give yourself one point for each dot that it touches.

- Number 2. Use your pencil and ruler to connect the two green dots that have red circles around them. (pause) If the line you just made crosses the first line you made, give yourself two points.

- Number 3. Use your pencil to draw a small circle around any one of the green dots. (pause) Now, use your ruler to draw a straight line between the dot with the circle you just drew and the big orange dot. (pause) Give yourself one point for each box your line goes through.

- Number 4. Look at the black dots. Give yourself one point for every black dot which is all the way inside a box which touches the outside edge of the paper (Boxes 1, 2, 3, 4, 8, 12, 16, etc.).

- Number 5. Now, give yourself one point for every black dot which is all the way inside any even-numbered box.

- Number 6. Look at your black dots again. If you can connect three black dots to make a triangle without crossing any of the lines you have already drawn, do it, and give yourself three points.

- Number 7. Give yourself one point for each black dot which touches a fold line.

- Number 8. Use your pencil and ruler to connect the brown dot and the orange dot. Give yourself one point for each pencil line (not fold line) your new line crosses.

Now, let's see who has the most points. Add up your scores and we'll find out how lucky you were today.

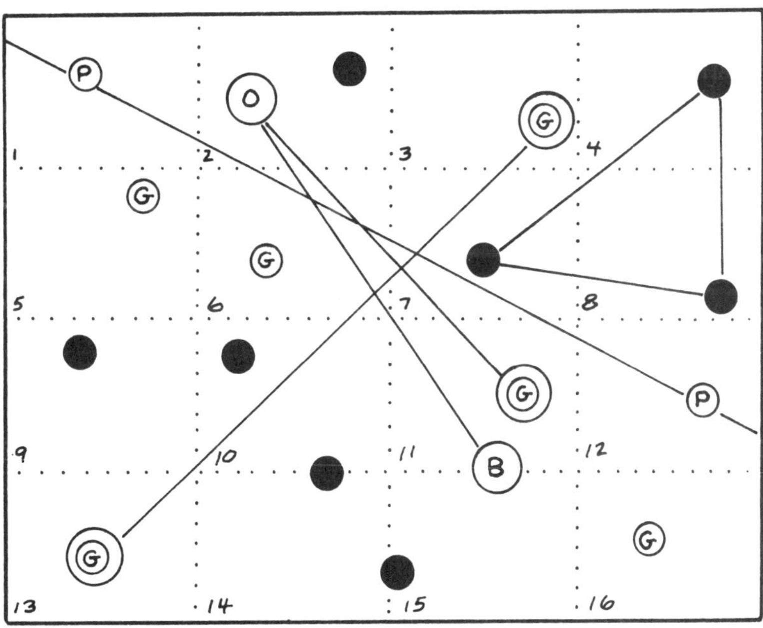

COLORS GREEN, PURPLE, BROWN AND ORANGE INDICATED BY G-P-B-O. BLACK DOTS SHOWN BLACK. CIRCLES AROUND "G" DOTS WOULD BE RED.

Lucky Dots and Lines (2)

About this activity...

Here is a slightly more sophisticated version. Note that Instruction 6 provides an opportunity for students to exercise a touch of good judgment to increase their score.

Materials needed...

Plain paper, pencil, crayons, ruler.

Directions to students...

Are you ready for another "Lucky Dots and Lines" game?

I have given you two pieces of paper. You will also need a pencil, your crayons and a ruler.

First, use your pencil to number 1-8 on one of your pieces of paper, starting with number one and going down to number eight. Set that paper aside when you are finished.

Now, on the blank sheet of paper, use your pencil to draw 20 little circles. Make them about the size of a pea, and spread them out all across the paper. (pause) Next, make four bigger circles — about the size of your thumbnail — anywhere on your paper.

Next, we need to make some folds, but this time we'll be making just two. First, fold the paper — the one with the circles — in half. Press down on the fold to make it good and sharp. Leave your paper folded, and then fold it in half in the other direction.

Open up your paper and spread it out. You should see four boxes made by the fold marks.

Place the piece of paper with one of its long sides closest to you. Number the top left-hand box "1," the top right-hand box "2," the bottom left-hand box "3," and the bottom right-hand box "4."

Now, we need to do some coloring. First, I want you to color any ten of the little circles red. (pause) Color the other ten little circles blue. (pause) Finally, color the four big circles orange.

Next, I want you to make some lines. You will be drawing six lines in all. None of them should cross or touch each other. First, find two blue dots that are close together and use your pencil and ruler to draw a straight line between them. Do the same thing with two other pairs of blue dots. (pause) Next, draw a straight line between two red dots that are close together. (pause) Do the same thing with two other pairs of red dots.

Now, we're ready to see how lucky you are today.

- Number 1. How many of the lines you made are completely inside of a box — any box? Give yourself one point for every line that doesn't cross over into another box or touch a fold line. Put the number next to number one on your score sheet.

- Number 2. If you have one or more lines that touch two boxes, give yourself two points. If you don't, give yourself a zero.

- Number 3. Draw straight lines connecting all four orange dots so that you make a four-sided figure. It's okay if these four lines cross other lines you have drawn. (pause) How many little dots did you capture in the middle of the shape you just drew? Give yourself one point for each one.

- Number 4. How many of the lines you drew to connect the pairs of red dots and pairs of blue dots now cross the lines you drew to connect the orange dots? Count them and give yourself a point for every one of these lines.

- Number 5. Which of the four boxes holds the most dots which are not connected by lines? If it is Box 1, give yourself one point; if it is Box 2, give yourself two points; if it is Box 3, give yourself three points; if it is Box 4, give yourself four points. If there is a tie, use the higher box number for your score.

- Number 6. Now, for this question, you will be making just one straight line with your ruler. What is the greatest number of lines you can cross by drawing a straight line between any two dots that are not now connected? Remember, it has to be a straight line. Here's a hint: Use your ruler to try out different possibilities before you draw. Give yourself one point for every line your straight line crosses.

- Number 7. Now, look at the center of your paper — the place where the two folds meet. Find the dot that is closest to that place. If it is a big orange dot, give yourself five points; if it is a red dot, give yourself three points; if it is a blue dot, give yourself one point.

- Number 8. Is there at least one unconnected dot in each of the four boxes? If there is, give yourself four points. If there is not, you get a zero.

Now, the time has come to add up your points. Who is the lucky winner today?

COLORS RED, BLUE AND ORANGE ARE INDICATED BY R-B-O.

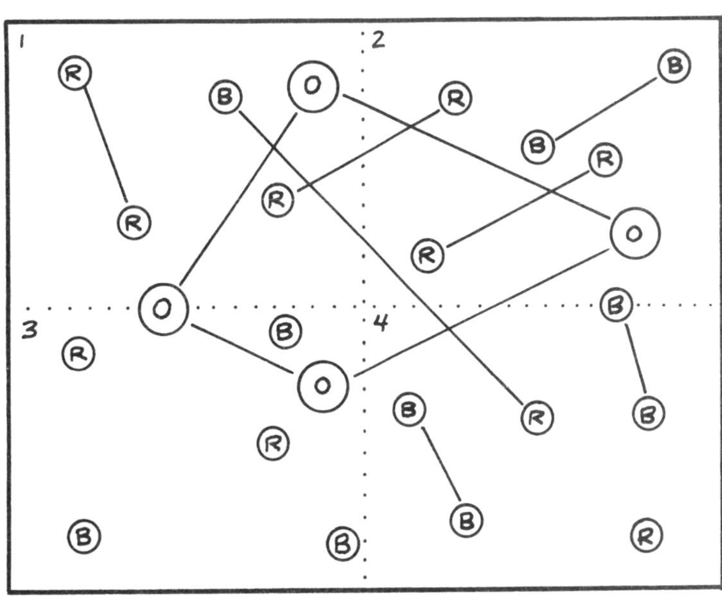

Up in the Air

About this activity...

The directions in this assignment are very precise. Notice, however, that children have not been told how to draw a kite, a cloud, a bird, etc. Proper placement in the boxes provides the listening and direction-following challenge.

Materials needed...

Plain paper, pencil.

Directions to students...

We are going to have some fun with today's activity. It is called "Up in the Air." I'll tell you about it in a minute, but first we have to get ready.

First, fold your paper in half across the short side. Press down on the fold to make it sharp.

Leave your paper folded, and fold it in half again the other way. Crease the fold again. Then fold it in half one more time in the other direction.

Now, open up your paper and smooth it out. You will notice that you have made eight rectangles.

Turn your paper so that one of its long sides is facing you. Number the rectangles 1-8, starting with the upper left-hand rectangle, and going across to the right. The lower left-hand rectangle will be Number 5.

All right. Now, we're ready to get started, so listen carefully. First, draw a line all the way across the bottom of your paper. Make your line as far from the bottom of the paper as your thumb is wide.

Now, we're going to think of the line you just drew as the ground. Everything above the line will be the sky. By the time you are finished, there are going to be a lot of things up in the sky... or I guess you could say "up in the air," because certain things will be close to the ground.

Now, do everything I say, and try to do it quickly.

- Look! There is an airplane. It is in the top half of Rectangle 1 and it is flying from left to right. Draw it.
- Draw some clouds in the top part of Rectangles 2 and 3.
- The sun is peeking out from behind the clouds in Rectangle 2. Draw it.
- It must be spring, because someone is flying a kite. Draw the kite in the bottom half of Rectangle 4.
- The kite's string goes down to the ground through Rectangles 8 and 7. Draw it.
- Oh, oh! I see 10 mosquitoes near the ground in Rectangle 6. Show them by making 10 little dots.

- Too bad! Someone has lost a balloon. It is floating up into the air. Right now it's in the bottom half of Rectangle 1. There is a short string attached to it. Go ahead and draw the balloon.
- Now, someone has shot an arrow at the balloon! The arrow is traveling toward the balloon. Right now it is in the top right-hand corner of Rectangle 5. Show us what it looks like. Remember, it is headed directly toward the balloon.
- Would you believe this? A small bird has landed on the kite! It must be tired. Draw a little bird taking a rest on the kite.
- Now, I see three birds flying near one of the clouds in Rectangle 3. They are very far away. Draw them.
- Someone has thrown a baseball into the air. Right now it is in the middle of Rectangle 6. Draw it.
- The person who threw the ball is not in our picture. That person is standing on the ground just outside the left-hand edge of Rectangle 5. Draw a dotted line between the lower left-hand side of Rectangle 5 and the ball you just drew to show the direction from which it was thrown.
- Wait a minute! This is impossible! What is your first name doing up in the air? Write your first name in the middle of Rectangle 8. Make it fairly small.
- Oh, I see! Your name is on a sign that is being held up by a long stick. Draw the outline of the sign around your name. Draw the stick, also.
- Now, we have come to the end. There is a swarm of smart little bees flying in Rectangle 7. You can tell they are smart, because they have spelled out the words, "The End." Use dots to show how that would look.

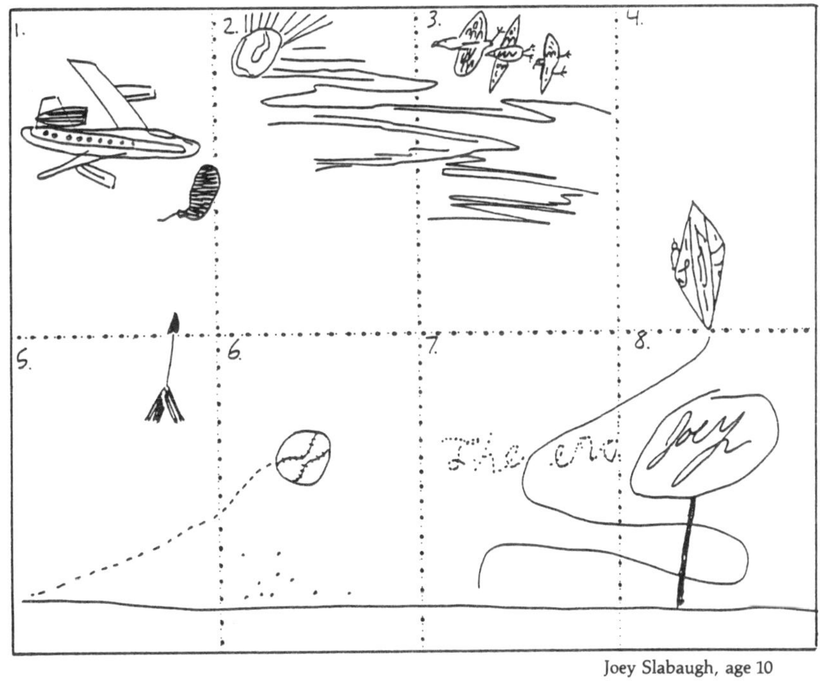

Joey Slabaugh, age 10

DOTTED LINES INDICATE FOLDS.

Under the Water

About this activity...

The art in this activity is really incidental. The positioning is the real point.

Materials needed...

Plain paper, pencil.

Directions to students...

We are now going to do an activity called "Under the Water." It is a lot like the "Up in the Air" activity we have done, so I think you are going to enjoy it.

Let's begin by getting a piece of paper ready. First, fold the paper in half across the short side. Press down on the fold to make it good and sharp.

Leave your paper folded, and fold it in half again the other way. Crease the fold again. Then, fold it in half one more time in the other direction.

Now, open up your paper and smooth it out. You will notice that you have made eight rectangles.

Next, turn your paper so that one of its long sides is facing you. Number the rectangles 1-8, starting with the upper left-hand rectangle and going across to the right. The lower left-hand rectangle will be Number 5. Put the numbers in the lower left-hand corner of the rectangle.

Good. Now, we're ready to get on with the fun part. Since this activity is called "Under the Water," we need some water. Let's start by making a line that looks like waves all the way across your paper. Draw the line about halfway up in Rectangles 1, 2, 3 and 4.

Okay. From now on we're going to think of everything below the line as "under the water," and everything above the line as "above the water." Now, do everything I say and do it fairly quickly.

- Draw a little boat floating on the water in Rectangle 2.
- There is a person sitting in the boat. The person is holding a fishing pole. Draw the person and the pole.
- Now, draw a fishing line that goes from the end of the pole all the way down through Rectangle 2 and halfway down into Rectangle 6.
- At the end of the line, draw a fishhook with a worm on it.
- Inside Rectangle 6, draw a big fish looking at the worm. It must be a smart fish, because its mouth is closed. Make sure the fish doesn't touch Rectangles 5 or 7.
- Three little fish are swimming in the middle of Rectangle 8. Draw them.
- Draw a big fish which is about ready to chase them. Put it in Rectangle 8 also.

- There are three little bubbles above each of the three little fish. The bubbles are floating toward the top of the rectangle. Draw them.
- Six pieces of seaweed are growing up from the bottom of Rectangle 5. The longest piece reaches up to about the middle of the rectangle. Please draw them.
- Look! There is an octopus! It is floating in the water above the seaweed. Draw its head in Rectangle 1 and its eight tentacles in Rectangle 5.
- Draw three seagulls flying in the air in Rectangle 3.
- The sun has appeared near the top of Rectangle 2. Draw it.
- The person in the boat doesn't want to get a sunburn and has put on a hat. Draw the hat.
- A fish has jumped all the way out of the water in Rectangle 4. Show how it would look.
- Now, a little fish is looking at the worm in Rectangle 6. Draw it with its mouth open.
- And now we know why the fish has jumped out of the water in Rectangle 4. There is a shark under the water in that rectangle. Draw the shark.
- What's going on in Rectangle 7? Not much. Draw a couple of clams near the bottom of the rectangle.
- Now, I see a duck! It is floating in the water in Rectangle 1. Draw the duck.
- I forgot to tell you that the boat in Rectangle 2 has an anchor. It is on the bottom in Rectangle 6, and there is a rope that runs from the anchor all the way to the boat. Draw the anchor and the rope.
- My goodness, I must be seeing things! I see a big bubble in Rectangle 7. The bubble has your first name in it. Try to show how that would look.

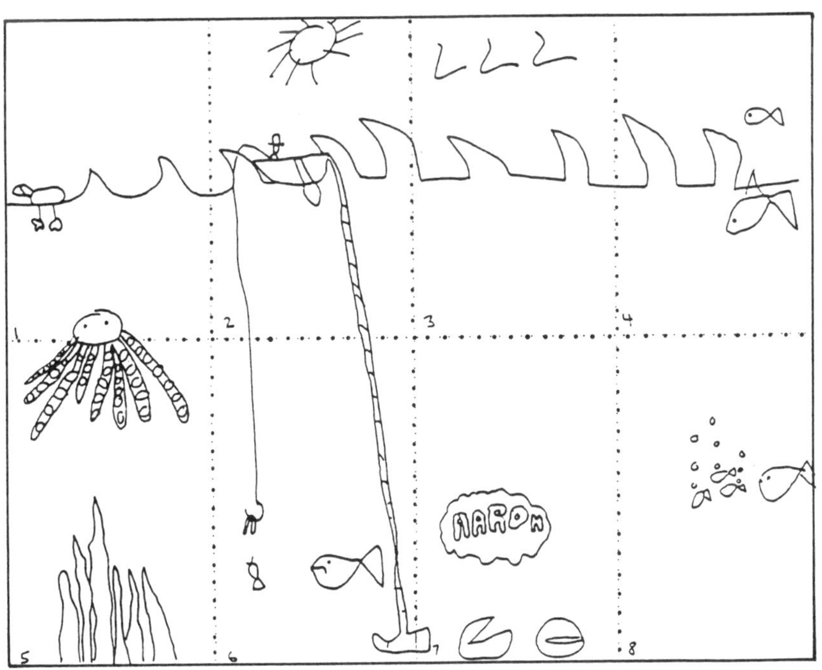

Aaron Van Scoy, age 11

Moving Colors

About this activity...

Here's a change of pace with lots of action. You'll find the excitement (and possibly the frustration level) building as you pick up the tempo. The activity can be repeated many times with good direction-following dividends.

Materials needed...

Strip of paper (divide 8½″ × 11″ sheet of paper into three vertical pieces), crayons.

Directions to students...

This is a game called "Moving Colors." In order to play, you must follow directions very well. You must also make your own game pieces, so let's get started.

Tear the strip of paper I have given you into four pieces. Try to make each piece about the same size. Do this now.

Next, take out your crayons. Put a big red dot on one of the pieces of paper. Now, put a big blue dot on another one of the pieces. Make a big orange dot on another piece. Finally, make a green dot on the last piece.

Put your crayons away. Now we're ready to play the game.

> First, put the pieces of paper in a row going across your desk. Put the red dot on your left, the orange dot next, then the blue dot, and then the green dot.
>
> Now, here is something you need to remember: Red is now in a place we will call Place 1, orange is in Place 2, blue is in Place 3, and green is in Place 4. It's easy to remember, because you are counting from left to right.
>
> Now, we are going to put the colors into a different order. Make sure you remember the numbering rules I just explained to you. Place 1 is always on the left, then Place 2, then Place 3. Place 4 is always on the right.
>
> Let's start by practicing. When I give you a color and a number, I want you to move that one piece of paper to the proper place. For example, if I said, "red—2," you would move the red piece to the second place. This would mean that orange is now in Place 1. Okay, do that. Put the red piece in Place 2. Notice that you have to move the orange piece over a little bit to make room for the red piece. That's something you'll have to be doing all the time as we play. Your order should now be: orange—1, red—2, blue—3 and green—4. Understand? Remember, you never change the order of more than one piece at a time. The only thing you do with the other pieces is to move them to make room for the piece you are changing.
>
> If I now say, green—1, what would you do? You would just have to move the green all the way to the left. Do that now. Now, your order should be: green—1, orange—2, red—3 and blue—4.

Do you have the idea? Okay, let's start. I'll give you several instructions and we'll see if we all end up in the same place. Here goes.

orange—4
blue—4
red—3
green—2

Now, let's see how you did. If you followed directions, you should now have orange in Place 1, then green, red and blue. Do you? If you don't, arrange them that way — orange, green, red, blue — and listen more closely next time. Let's try again.

red—1
red—4
red—1
orange—4
blue—1

Now, what order should you have? Yes, blue, red, green and orange.

All right, now I'm going to give you a really long list and we'll see how you do. (Note: Read from top to bottom of left column first and follow that pattern on to the right.)

blue—2	green—1	orange—4	orange—1
blue—4	blue—2	green—4	green—3
orange—1	red—1	blue—4	blue—1
red—3	green—4	red—4	orange—4
green—3	blue—1	green—1	red—2

Okay, we're finished. What do you have now? Yes, you should have blue, red, green, orange.

Now, let's go even faster! You should be starting with blue, red, green and orange. (Note: Begin again from top left.)

orange—2	orange—4	red—3	blue—1
blue—4	blue—4	green—3	orange—3
green—4	orange—4	blue—4	red—3
red—1	red—4	red—2	blue—4
green—3	blue—1	orange—1	orange—2

If you followed directions, you should now have green, orange, red and blue.

The Triangle-ope

About this activity...

You and your students will have fun comparing drawings after this activity is finished. It should come as a surprise to students that such a simple, straightforward set of descriptive statements can produce such varied results.

Materials needed...

Plain paper, pencil.

Directions to students...

Back in the days before cameras were invented, the only way you could show someone how something looked was to draw a picture of it. Today, we are going to pretend we are living in those times. We are going to imagine we have just received a letter from an explorer who has discovered a strange animal. The explorer has not sent a drawing, just the letter. It is going to be your job to draw a picture of the animal described in the letter. Remember, we're just pretending, so the animal is going to be really fantastic. By the way, the explorer has named the animal a "Triangle-ope." You'll see why in a minute.

I will now read the part of the letter that tells about the "Triangle-ope." I'll read each sentence slowly, and I will give you some time between sentences. Your job is to go ahead and draw what is described in each sentence.

- The animal has a body shaped like a big triangle.
- Its head is shaped like a bumpy circle.
- It has long legs, and each of its feet has three toes with a claw on the end of each toe.
- Its tail is very long and covered with fur.
- Its body has four large spots and three smaller spots.
- Its eyes are large.
- Its mouth is small.
- So is its nose.
- I noticed two long, curved horns on the top of its head.

Well, that's the end of the letter. Let's see how the creature you drew looks.

Debbie Baldwin, age 10

The Face of B-5

About this activity...

This activity gets off to an inventive start by asking children to draw around their own fists. After that, they must listen carefully to your description of a friendly little alien named B-5. There are rules here... but there is still plenty of room for the imagination.

Materials needed...

Plain paper, pencil.

Directions to students...

Do you remember the letter from the explorer who had seen a "Triangle-ope?" Well, let's pretend I have just received a letter from someone who is writing a story. The story is about a cute little creature who drops in from outer space for a visit on Planet Earth. The creature's name is B-5, and it is very friendly. The person who is writing the story did not send a picture of B-5 with this letter. However, the author's letter *did* give a description of B-5's face.

I will now read the part of the letter that tells about B-5. I'll read each sentence slowly, and I will give you some time between sentences. Your job is to go ahead and draw what is described in each sentence.

- B-5's head is lumpy and bumpy. The best way to draw the shape of its head is to place your fist on a piece of paper and draw all the way around it, starting at one side of your wrist and going all the way around to the other side.
- B-5 has a very wide mouth, which is always smiling.
- It has straight hair, which sticks straight up.
- Its eyes are small and round.
- It has very large, dark eyebrows.
- B-5's nose is long and skinny, starting between its eyes and reaching almost all the way down to its mouth.
- Its ears are quite large, and come to points on the top.
- B-5 always wears a little bow tie around its neck.

That's the end of the letter. Let's see your picture of B-5.

Michael Thompson, age 9

A Postcard from Pluton

About this activity...

Drawing a tall house with a pointed roof is easy. However, by the time students figure out how to fit a "Plutonite" helicopter into their composition, they will have performed some rigorous mental gymnastics.

Materials needed...

Plain paper, pencil.

Directions to students...

Let's pretend that today I have received a postcard dated 2,099. The postcard is from a friend who has gone to a planet named Pluton for a vacation. The card says that the people on Pluton are called Plutonites, and that they live in very strange houses.

I will now read the part of the card that tells about the Plutonite houses. I will read each sentence slowly, and I will give you some time between sentences. Your job is to go ahead and draw what is described in each sentence.

- A Plutonite house is tall and has a pointed roof.
- The front of the house has three doors — a tall one for adults, a medium-sized one for children, and a very small one for pets.
- There are three round windows near the top of the house.
- Since Plutonite children are very curious, you can usually see a couple of them peeking out of the round windows.
- All Plutonite houses have two tall, skinny trees in the front yard.
- There are many large birds on Pluton. You can see a bird at the top of every tree.
- The Plutonites decorate their doors with stars. Adults' doors have three stars, children's doors have two stars and pets' doors have one star.
- In front of every Plutonite house there is a little helicopter which the family uses for going to work and for shopping.

That's the end of the postcard. The card ends with the word, "goodle-borp," which is Plutonian for "good-bye." Now, let's see what kind of pictures you drew.

Michael Thompson, age 9

The Moving Line

About this activity...

The first time you run through this activity, you may have trouble keeping students from going too rapidly. Stress that they should keep a slow, even pace. The circle "stall" should help to keep everyone in sync. Try watching one student draw as you give the instructions.

Materials needed...

Plain paper, pencil.

Directions to students...

Our activity today is called "The Moving Line." It is called that because your pencil will *always* be moving during the activity. You will *always* be making a line of some sort.

Here is how the activity works: I will be telling you what kind of line to make, and where the line should go. If you get to the place I tell you to go *before* I have given another direction, keep your pencil moving by going around and around in a tight little circle. Understand?

First, let's try a warm-up activity. Start by putting a little number "1" in the upper left-hand corner of your paper. Put a "2" in the upper right-hand corner, a "3" in the lower left-hand corner, and a "4" in the lower right-hand corner.

Now, starting near Number 1, slowly make a line over to Number 2. Remember, if you get to Number 2 before I give the next direction, just go around in little circles. All right, now make a light line all the way to the middle of the paper (pause)and then make a dark line down to Number 4. (pause) Finally, make a wiggly line over to Number 3.(pause) Are you still going around in circles? You should be! All right, now you can stop.

Let's try it again. Turn your paper over and number it the same way you did before. (pause) Remember, you don't have to do this activity perfectly. You may make some mistakes. That's okay. But do your best, because this is good practice in listening and direction-following.

All set? Put your pencil near Number 2, and here we go!

- Make a light, wiggly line down to Number 3.
- When you reach Number 3, go around in circles a few times and then make a straight line to the middle of the paper.
- Now, head very slowly for Number 4, making eight small loops along the way, and then making the rest of the line straight.
- Make a dark line straight up to Number 2.

- Come back down to Number 4, using a very light line next to the dark line.
- Now, go over to Number 3 with a heavy, jagged line.
- Next, let your line wander slowly all over the paper — anywhere you want to go — while I count to five. (Count out loud to five, counting slowly.)
- All right, now trace your way back along the wandering line you just made. Trace back until you reach Number 3. (Pause until everyone has reached Number 3 and is making circles.)
- Now, use a very light line to go up to Number 1.
- Make a line of big loops all the way over to Number 2.
- Make a straight line halfway back to Number 1.
- Then, go down to the middle.
- When you reach the middle, go around in a little circle. Keep going around, making your circles larger and larger until you run out of paper. Then STOP!

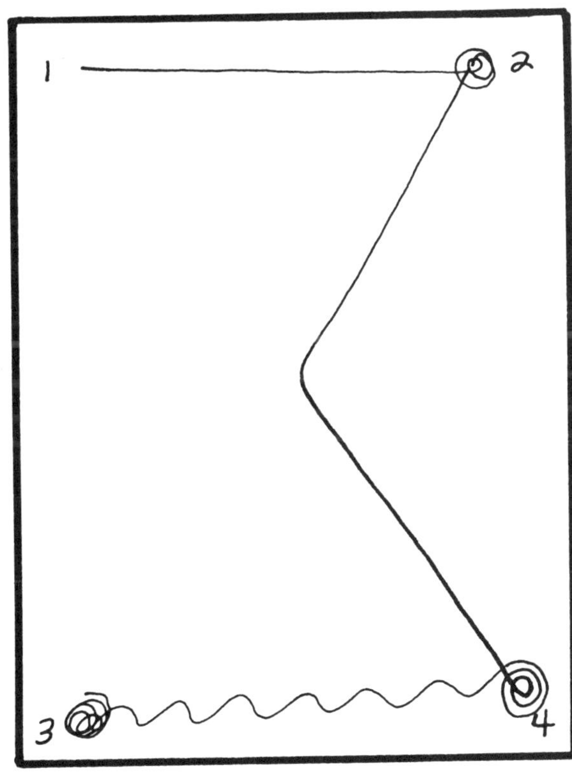

THE PRACTICE ACTIVITY.

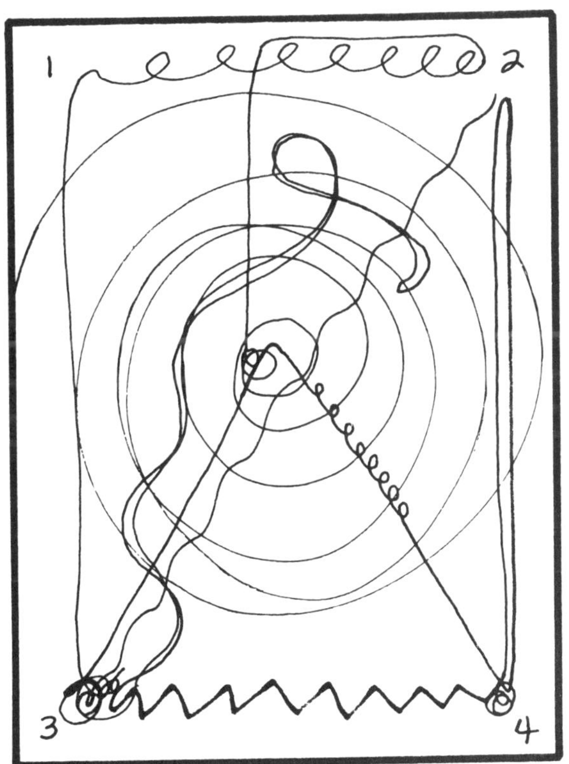

THE LONGER VERSION. THIS ACTIVITY CAN BE DONE WITH THE PAPER PLACED EITHER HORIZONTALLY OR VERTICALLY.

The Moving Line (2)

About this activity...

The rule change alters this activity significantly. By now children will probably have a feel for the rate at which they should be drawing.

Materials needed...

Plain paper, pencil.

Directions to students...

We are going to try another "Moving Line" activity today, but we will be doing things a little differently.

One thing will not change: You must keep your pencil moving at all times. Just make little circles if you finish doing something before I have given another direction.

Now, for the changes: You can draw anywhere at all on the paper. You will be following my directions, but *where* you put your lines will be up to you. BUT... unless you are making little circles or loops, your lines cannot touch or cross each other. If you run out of room and cannot follow my directions without touching or crossing a line you have already made, just stop drawing and fold your hands on your desk.

Do you have it? Keep your line moving at all times... draw anywhere you wish... don't touch or cross lines you have already drawn.

All right, let's try a practice activity so we can get acquainted with the new rules.

- Start near the middle of your paper and slowly draw a line in any direction.
- Now, make three loops.
- Now, draw a straight line.
- Change directions and draw another straight line.
- Make 10 zig-zags in any direction.
- Make 12 loops in any direction.
- Draw a line all the way around everything you have drawn so far.
- Stop.

Were you able to do it? I think you can see that it is a good idea to keep your lines fairly short so that you do not run out of paper too quickly. All right, turn your papers over and follow these directions.

- Start in the middle and head for one corner.
- Make 10 loops in any direction.
- Make a straight line.
- Change directions and make another straight line.
- Go down.
- Go across.
- Go up.
- Go down.
- Make a curving line.
- Make three loops.
- Make five wiggles.
- Now, draw a line around everything you have drawn so far.
- Next, go to all four corners of the paper.
- Make six more loops.
- Make six straight lines that go in different directions.
- Make a short, wiggly line.
- Go down.
- Go over.
- Go up.
- Stop. Draw a star. You are finished!

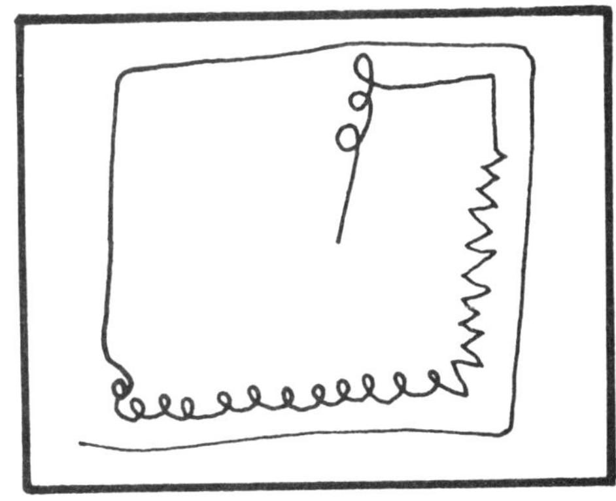

THE PRACTICE ACTIVITY.

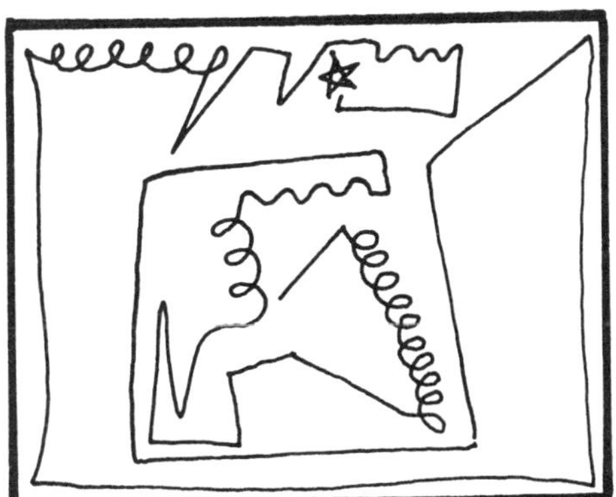

THE LONGER VERSION.

Build a Message

About this activity...

Your instructions tell children how to construct letters that spell out a message. The message itself is unimportant. The purpose of this activity is to encourage students to react to some very carefully crafted instructions.

Materials needed...

Worksheet (see illustration), pencil.

Directions to students...

We are now going to do an activity called "Build a Message." I'll be giving you directions which you must follow carefully to make some letters of the alphabet. You will be making one capital letter in each box. There is one rule: None of the marks you make should touch the edge of the box.

Are you ready? Here are your directions.

- In Box 2, make a straight up-and-down line in the middle of the box. It should start just above the bottom line and go almost all of the way to the top line.
- Do the same thing in Box 3.
- In Box 4, make a straight up-and-down line near the left-hand edge of the box. It should almost — but not quite — touch the top and the bottom of the box.
- Do the same thing in Boxes 1, 5, 6 and 7. (Pause between numbers.)
- Now, in Box 1, you need to draw another straight up-and-down line exactly as long as the one that is already there. Only this time, draw it so that it is very close to the right-hand side of the box.
- Do the same thing in Box 4.
- Now, in Box 6, make a dot in the middle of the up-and-down line.
- In Box 5, you'll be drawing a line about half as long as the line you have already drawn there. It should start at the top of the up-and-down line and go straight across toward the right... not too far. Remember, it should be only about half as long as the up-and-down line.
- Do the same thing in Box 7.
- Now, go back to Box 1. Make a dot in the middle of the up-and-down line on the left. (pause) Make another dot in the middle of the up-and-down line on the right.

- Do the same thing in Box 4.
- Look at Box 6. Make a letter "P" by drawing a half circle that uses the top half of the line as the side of the half circle. The straight side of the half circle should go down only as far as the center dot.
- Next, go to Box 5. I want you to make another short line. Make it the same length as the short line you have already drawn there. It should start at the very bottom of the up-and-down line and go straight across in the same direction as the other short line.
- Do the same thing in Box 7.
- Now, draw a straight line between the two dots in Box 1.
- Do the same thing in Box 4.
- Next, go to Box 5. There is really just one capital letter we can make by using the lines that are already there. What is it? (Discuss, and direct children to make an "E" in Boxes 5 and 7.)
- Now, put a line across the top of the up-and-down line in Box 3. Pretend you're balancing it on top of the up-and-down line, with half of the new line on each side.
- Is "THEPE" a word? What do you think the message is supposed to say? (Discuss until children decide Box 6 must contain an "R.")

THE WORKSHEET. MAKE SURE BOXES ARE SQUARE AND NUMBERED AS SHOWN HERE.

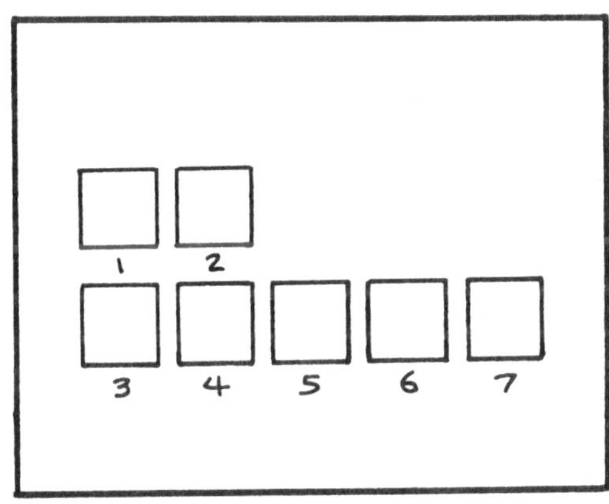

THE SOLUTION.

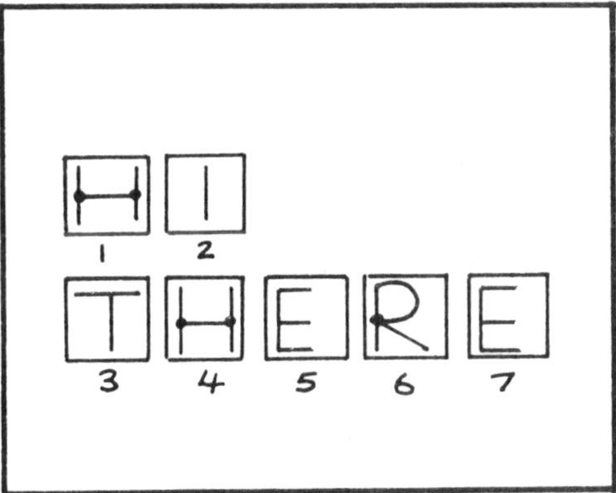

Build a Message (2)

About this activity...

Anyone with the patience to follow this complex set of directions deserves a treat! Provide one.

Materials needed:

Worksheet (see illustration), pencil, treat.

Directions to students...

Today, we are going to do another "Build a Message" activity. The message will be longer than the first one we did, which just spelled out the words, "HI THERE." But I think you will like this message, so be sure to listen and follow directions carefully.

Remember, you'll be making one capital letter in each box. None of the marks you make should touch the edge of the box.

Before we start, I'd like to ask you one favor. If you figure out what the message says before we are finished, please don't say it out loud. Okay? Are you ready? Here we go.

- In Box 2, make a straight, up-and-down line in the middle of the box. It should start just above the bottom line and go almost all the way to the top line.
- Do the same thing in Boxes 1, 9, and 13. (Pause between numbers.)
- Put a dot right in the middle of Box 3.
- Now, in Box 8, you'll be making a triangle. But first listen to all of my instructions. The triangle should be in the top half of the box. All of its sides should be about equal in length. Its sides should be about half as long as the lines that form the sides of the box. The top point of the triangle should point straight up. The bottom side of the triangle should go in the same direction as the bottom edge of the box. Okay. Go ahead and draw the triangle. When you are finished, do the same thing in Box 12. (Read twice if necessary.)
- Now, make a big letter "C" in the left-hand side of Box 6.
- In Box 4, make a straight up-and-down line near the left-hand edge of the box. It should almost touch the top and the bottom of the box. (pause) Do the same thing in Boxes 3, 5, 7, 10 and 11. (Pause between numbers.)
- Now, in Box 4, you'll be drawing a line about half as long as the line you have already drawn there. It should start in the middle of the up-and-down line and go straight across toward the right... not too far. Remember, it should be only about half as long as the up-and-down line. (pause) Do the same thing in Boxes 5 and 11.

- Now, in Box 3, you are to draw another up-and-down line exactly as long as the one that is already there. Only this time, draw it so that it is very close to the right-hand side of the box.
- Next, go back to Box 4. This time I want you to make another short line. Make it the same length as the short line you have already drawn. It should start at the very top of the up-and-down line and go in the same direction as the other short line . . . straight across. (pause) Do the same thing in Boxes 5 and 11.
- Now, in Box 7, make a dot in the middle of the up-and-down line. Do the same thing in Box 10.
- Now, go back to Box 3. Draw a straight line from the top of the up-and-down line on the left to the dot in the middle.
- Let's go to Box 7. Make a letter "P" by drawing a half circle that uses the top half of the line as the side of the half circle. The straight side of the half circle should go down only as far as the center dot. After you are finished, do the same thing in Box 10.
- Now, in Box 8, turn the triangle you have drawn there into the letter "A" by adding two more lines. Do the same thing in Box 12.
- Go to Box 6. Turn the letter "C" into the letter "O."
- In Box 1, draw one more line to make the letter "T." (pause) Do the same thing in Boxes 9 and 13.
- In Box 4, use one more line to make the letter "E." (pause) Do the same thing in Box 11.

You have just three more lines to make to complete the message. Can you do it? (Discuss and eat!)

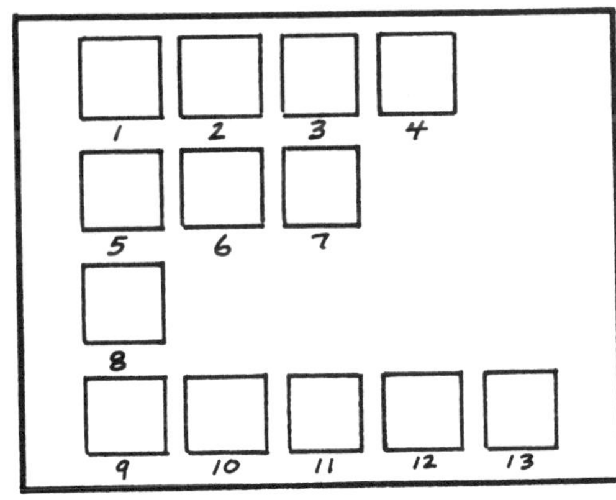

WORKSHEET WITH SQUARE BOXES.

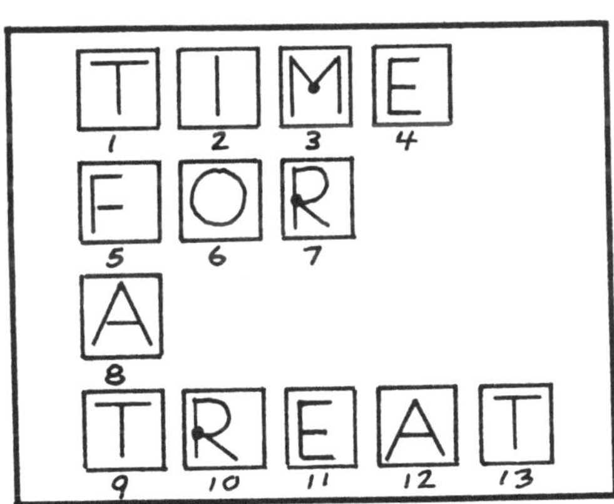

THE FINISHED "MESSAGE."

A Tear-able Mystery

About this activity...

The real direction-following here involves the tearing of the paper. After this has been done students are encouraged to use their imagination.

Materials needed...

One piece of 3-hole notebook paper, pencil.

Directions to students...

Our activity today is called "A Tear-able Mystery." Why? Because we are going to be doing some paper tearing, and because you will be following my instructions for quite a while before you know what you are doing.

Are you ready to get started with the mystery? Okay, first I want you to place your paper on your desk with the holes on the left.

Now, follow these instructions carefully.

- Your first job is to tear a small square from the top left-hand corner of the paper. The top hole should be inside the square. Your square doesn't have to be perfect, just do the best you can. Put a small number "1" on the little square and set it aside.
- Now, we get to the big piece. Starting at the corner where you just tore out the square, tear all the way down and across to the lower right-hand corner. Don't worry if the torn place is crooked... just try to end up at the lower right-hand corner.
- Write the number "2" on the piece that has no holes and set it aside.
- Write the number "3" on the other piece... the one with the holes.
- Now, fold Piece 3 so that one hole is exactly on top of the other. Crease the fold so the paper stays flat. Then, set it aside.
- Next, pick up Piece 2 and make a fold somewhere near the center of the piece.
- Now, still working with Piece 2, tear out a small chunk of paper from a place near the middle of the fold you just made. Try to tear out a shape like a half circle so you will have a round hole when you open up the paper. Your hole should be about the size of a quarter. Crumple up the little piece you just tore out and set it aside. You won't be needing it.

Now, let's get back to the mystery. We have made three pieces of paper, and we have numbered them 1-3. Each of the pieces is quite different. In fact, they are *so* different that I know you won't guess what I'm going to ask you to do next.

I am now going to ask you to make... three heads! How? Just listen.

- First, find Piece 1, the smallest. I want you to use Piece 1 to make the head of a little person who is very surprised. Use the hole for the person's mouth. You may make any pencil marks you think you need.

- Next, unfold Piece 2. Your job is to make Piece 2 into the head of an imaginary animal. You can tear the paper in any way you wish, and you may make any pencil marks you want to make, but you *must* use the hole that is already there as the animal's eye.

- Now, pick up Piece 3. First, I will tell you that you must keep it folded. Don't open it up. This time I want you to turn the piece of paper into the head of a dog. Once again, you *must* use the hole for the eye. You cannot make any other tears in the paper. You *can* use your pencil to make any marks you want to make.

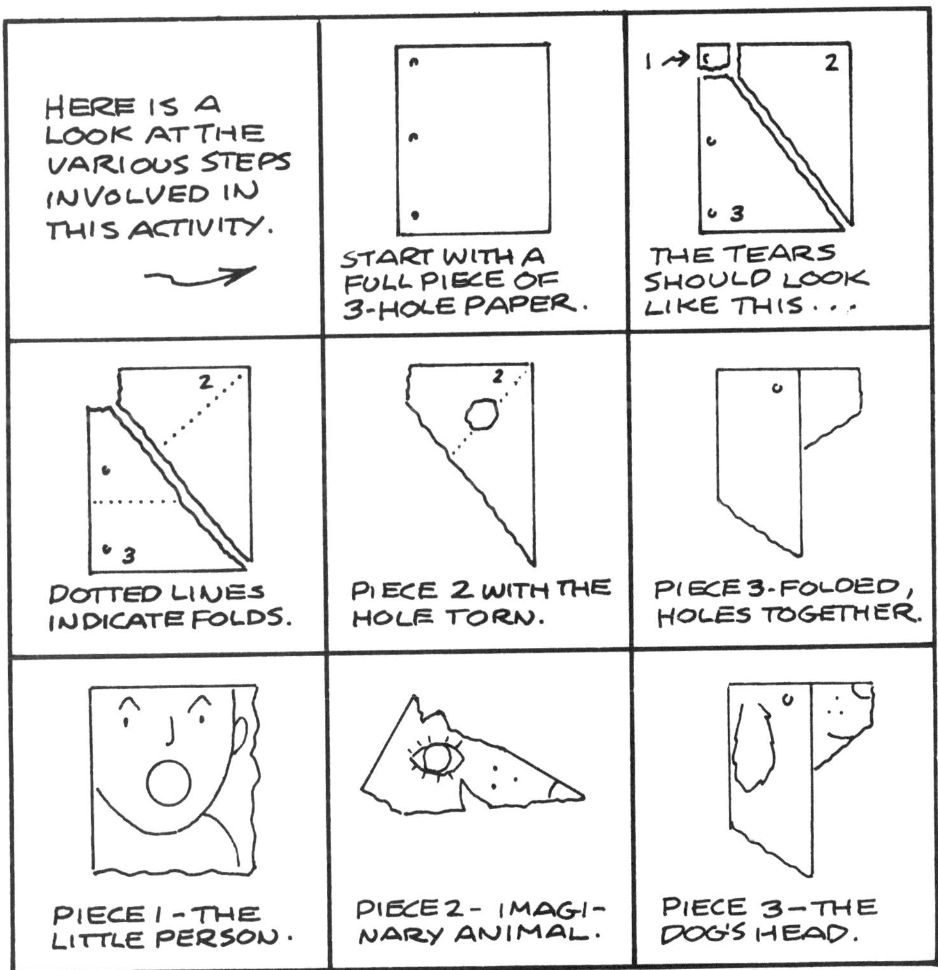

Stand Up, Sit Down

About this activity...

These stories are not Pulitzer Prize winners, but you'll get some good feedback about students' listening abilities as they react to the built-in cues. You can make the activity easier by emphasizing the italicized words, but give them a chance to do it the hard way first.

Materials needed...

None.

Directions to students...

Are you all tired of sitting down? Would you like to stretch your legs? Here's your chance. Today, we're going to play a listening game called "Stand Up, Sit Down." Here is how the game works.

I am going to read you three short stories. I will read each story all the way through once. Then, I will read it again more slowly, and this time you will be asked to stand up when you hear certain words and to sit down when you hear certain other words.

All right. Let's give it a try. Here's a story called "The Bike and the Stick." Let me read it to you first.

One day I was riding my *bike* along a sidewalk when I ran over a *stick* and fell down. I wasn't hurt, but everything I had in my pockets fell out. All of my *dimes* were scattered on the sidewalk and in the grass. I also dropped my new *pencil* and a bunch of *paper clips* I had been saving. I was so mad at the *stick* that I picked it up and threw it as far as I could. I guess I shouldn't have done that, because I almost hit a *car* that was passing by. I was afraid the driver would be mad, so I hid behind a *tree* until it had passed. Then I picked up my *paper clips* and my *pencil* and my *dimes* and rode home. And all of the way home, I watched for *sticks.*

Now that you have heard the story, here is what I want you to do. Every time you hear a word that describes something made out of metal, stand up. Remain standing until you hear a word that describes something made out of wood. Then, sit down. All right, now I'll read the story again. (Write: Up—Metal, Down—Wood on blackboard.)

Our next story is called "My Messy Brother." I'll read it first.

My little brother is the messiest eater I have ever seen. Just last night, we went out for hamburgers and the first thing he did was to drop his pickles onto the floor. Then he bit into his hamburger so hard that the *catsup* ran down all over his new yellow shirt. Another time not long ago, he couldn't get the *mustard* to come out of one of those squeeze bottles, so he just kept squeezing harder and harder. You know what happened next? The bottle was pointed at my dad, who was eating *straw-berries* at the time, and whoosh, a big glob of *mustard* hit him right on top of his head. And you ought to see my brother eat ice cream or marshmallows or even an *apple.* It's enough to ruin your appetite. Oh, yes, I guess I should also tell you about the time he put *butter* all over a *tomato* and ate it. Not only is he messy, he is crazy, too. Whoever heard of *butter* on a *tomato*? Next thing you know, he'll be pouring milk on oranges and carrots and lettuce and chocolate cake and green beans and *bananas*.

Here is your job this time: Every time you hear a word that describes a food that is red, stand up. Remain standing until you hear me mention a food which is yellow. Then, sit down. Now I'll read the story again. (Write: Up—Red Food, Down—Yellow Food on blackboard.)

Our third story today is called "The Hungry Ant."

Once a little *ant* was very hungry. "I need something sweet," it said to itself, "and I'll keep looking until I find something really good. Maybe I'll find a *watermelon* or a *marshmallow* or something in a *trash can*." As the *ant* crawled along, it just missed being stepped on by a *person*. It escaped from a *spider*, was almost trampled by a *dog*, and was nearly hit by a falling *acorn*. "Wow, the *world* is a dangerous place," said the *ant*. "Maybe I'll walk over to that *hill* and hide for a while. As the *ant* approached the *hill*, it noticed something strange. The *ant* smelled something very sweet, and also saw that the *hill* was a reddish color. What do you suppose the lucky *ant* had found? Was it really a *hill*? No, but to the *ant* it looked like a *hill*. Really, it was just a *gumdrop* some *boy* had dropped.

All right, this time I want you to think about size. Every time you hear a word that describes something smaller than an apple, stand up. Remain standing until you hear a word for something which is larger than an apple. Then, sit down. (Write: Up—Smaller than Apple, Down—Larger than Apple on blackboard.)

Stand Up, Sit Down (2)

About this activity...

This activity is tougher than the first "Stand Up, Sit Down" version, because the phonetic signals are harder to pick up than the conceptual clues. Enunciate!

Materials needed...

None.

Directions to students...

Today, we are going to play another "Stand Up, Sit Down" game. Let's go back over the rules.

I am going to read you three short stories. I will read each story all the way through once. Then I will read it again more slowly, and this time you will be asked to stand up when you hear certain words and to sit down when you hear certain other words.

Let's listen to the first story. It is called "Making Dumb Mistakes."

Have you ever had a *day* when everything seems to go wrong and you find yourself *making dumb mistakes?* I had one of those *days* recently. First, I climbed out of bed in the *morning* and put a sweater on backwards in the *dark. Mistake* number one! After that happened, I guess I was still *dreaming* or something, because I poured three times the amount of *milk* I needed on the cereal. I couldn't find anything but a *dishcloth* to use to clean up the *mess* on the floor. It took a long time, and I knew I would be late for school. So I ran, and because I was in such a hurry, I splashed through a huge puddle and soaked the new shoes I was wearing. At school, Mrs. *Davis* asked for the homework we were supposed to have finished the night before. I remembered I had left the paper at home on the fireplace *mantle.* Oh goodness, I thought, this *day* is never going to end. And you know, it was still only *morning.*

Now that you have heard the story, here is what you will be doing next. The last time you played this game, you were listening for things like color and size. This time you will be listening for words that begin with a certain letter. The letters for the first story are "D" and "M." Every time you hear a word that begins with a "D" you are to stand up. Remain standing until you hear a word that begins with an "M." Then, sit down. (Write: Up—D, Down—M on blackboard.)

Our next story is called "A Scare-Cut." Here it is.

Last fall, my *hair* was getting really shaggy. It *looked* so bad it reminded me of a *Halloween* wig. So I decided to go to a barber shop to get it cut. When I got there, I sat down in the chair and said to the barber, "*Look,* my *hair* is too *long.* Please cut it much shorter." The barber took out a *huge* pair of scissors and started cutting. Snip, snip, snip, snip went the scissors. The scissors snipped faster and faster and soon there was a *large* pile of *hair* on the floor. When the snipping finally stopped, I *looked* in the mirror. My *hair* was only about an inch *long*! "Shall I keep on snipping?" asked the barber. Just then I woke up and felt my *hair*. It was still *long* and I was *happy* that it had all been a dream.

Now, I will read the story again. This time, stand up every time you hear a word that begins with an "L." Remain standing until you hear a word that begins with an "H." Then, sit down. (Write: Up—L, Down—H on blackboard.)

Our last story today is called "The Colorful Shoes." Here it is.

One day I was in the school *cafeteria* eating my lunch with all the other students. I was using my *fork* and my knife to *cut* some beets which were *floating* in red juice when, to my surprise, the beets took off and landed right on my teacher's shoes. My teacher had just bought the shoes and they had *cost* her a lot of money. They had high heels and were very *fancy*. They had started out as a pretty *color* of blue, but now they were blue and beet-red. They really looked sort of *funny*, but I sure didn't laugh because I noticed a *crabby* expression on my teacher's *face*. "I'm sorry," I said. "The beets slid off my plate and I just *couldn't* help it." Her *frown* went away. She smiled and looked down at her shoes. "They really are *colorful* now," she said. "Blue and red are my *favorite colors*." I'm not sure she meant it, but it made me *feel* a lot better.

Okay. Now, I'll read the story again. Stand up any time you hear a word that begins with a "C," and sit down any time you hear a word that begins with an "F." (Write: Up—C, Down—F on blackboard.)

Cut-Ups!

About this activity...

Students will be turning one piece of notebook paper into 22 little pieces — if they follow your step-by-step directions carefully. This activity seems complicated, but is actually quite simple. It should be a confidence builder.

Materials needed...

One piece of 3-hole notebook paper, scissors, pencil.

Directions to students...

Our activity today is called "Cut-Ups." By the time you are finished, you will have snipped the piece of notebook paper I have given you into a lot of little pieces. How many? I won't tell! Finishing up with the correct number of pieces is part of the game.

Are you ready? Okay, first take out a pencil and your scissors.

- To begin, I want you to cut all the way along the up-and-down line that is nearest to the holes.
- Set the small piece aside. Now, fold the big piece of paper in half, with the fold going in the same direction as the lines. Open it up and cut all the way along the fold.
- Set one of the pieces aside. Find the up-and-down line on the other piece. When you find it, make a cut all the way along it.
- Now, mark the biggest piece of paper with a number "1" in one corner.
- Mark the next-to-the-biggest piece with a number "2." Put the number in one corner.
- Mark the long, thin piece without holes with a number "3" near one end.
- Okay. Now, pick up the long piece with the three holes. I want you to think of a way to use just one snip to make three pieces of paper with a hole in each piece. The pieces do not have to be the same size, but each piece *does* have to have a hole in it. (Note: Children may need to be given the hint that the paper must be folded in half to do this.)
- Your next job is to make one long, straight cut to divide Piece 1 into two triangles that are about the same size and shape. (Note: A diagonal cut from corner to corner is necessary. Give assistance if required.)
- Next, cut Piece 2 into four triangles of about the same size and shape.

- Your next job is easy. Cut Piece 3 into three pieces of about the same size.
- Now, look at all of the pieces you have made. Cut a narrow strip of paper from one of the two longest edges you can find. (Note: These will be found along the long sides of the triangle made from Piece 1.)
- Next, make two triangles out of *every* triangle you have made so far.
- Find the three little pieces you made from Piece 3. Cut each of them in half so that you make six little rectangles.
- Now, count all of the pieces you have made. Write the number on one of the pieces which has a hole. (pause) How many of you wrote the number "22?"

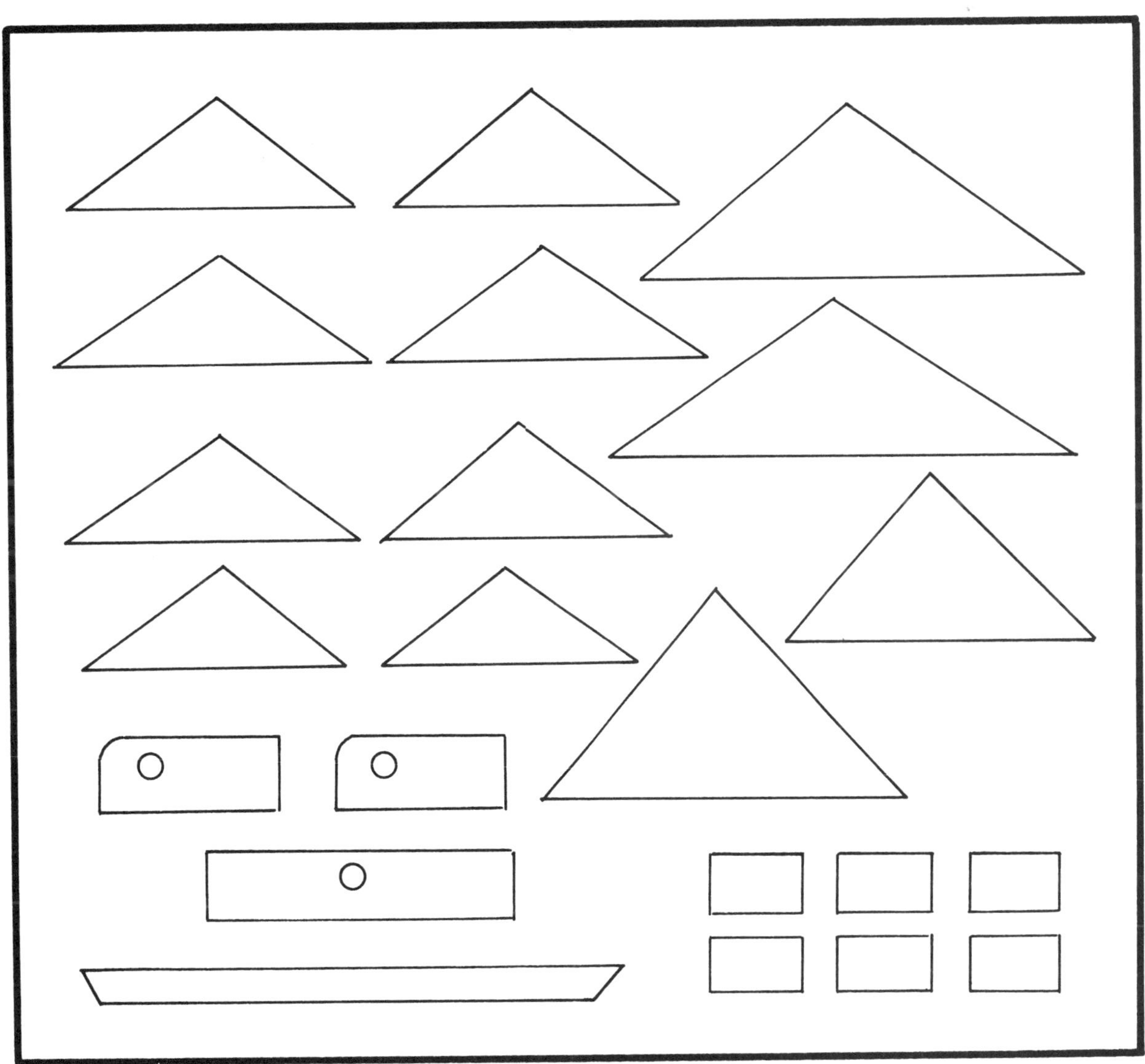

BY THE TIME STUDENTS ARE FINISHED, THEY SHOULD HAVE 22 LITTLE PIECES THAT LOOK SOMETHING LIKE THIS.

Build a Design

About this activity...

Here is a direction-following project with a real reward...an interesting piece of "modern art." After students have done all four activities in the "Build a Design" series, stage an impromptu art show and discuss the differences between the designs.

Materials needed...

Plain paper, pencil, crayons.

Directions to students...

Today, we are going to do an activity called, "Build a Design." I'm going to give you some directions which I want you to follow carefully, and the result should be a very interesting design.

First, place your paper so that one of the short sides is closest to you.

Now, using a pencil, I want you to make 20 dots — scatter them on the paper any way you like.

Next, number the dots 1-20. Put your numbers under the dots and keep the numbers small. It doesn't matter which dot gets which number.

Now, we're going to connect the dots with lines. I will be giving you two numbers at a time and you are going to be drawing a line between those dots. But here are two rules: Your lines cannot touch any other dots or numbers, and they cannot cross any other lines. That means most of your lines will have to be curved to avoid touching other lines or dots.

Here we go.

- Connect Dots 5 and 17.
- Connect Dots 6 and 10.
- Connect Dots 2 and 3.
- Connect Dots 8 and 15.
- Connect Dots 16 and 19.
- Connect Dots 4 and 11.
- Connect Dots 1 and 7.
- Connect Dots 9 and 14.
- Connect Dots 12 and 20.
- Connect Dots 13 and 18.

Now, we're going to change the rules. I'm going to be saying numbers again, but this time, you are going to be making a straight line between the dots, crossing whatever lines may be in the way.

Here we go.

- Connect Dots 5 and 12.
- Connect Dots 3 and 17.
- Connect Dots 9 and 10.
- Connect Dots 11 and 15.
- Connect Dots 18 and 20.
- Connect Dots 7 and 13.
- Connect Dots 1 and 6.
- Connect Dots 1 and 4.
- Connect Dots 14 and 15.
- Connect Dots 2 and 8.

Now, I want you to find one of the smaller shapes you have made — any shape that you like — and darken in the whole shape with your pencil.

Now, somewhere on your design where you think it would look nice, draw that same shape again and darken it in. Make it about the same size as the other shape.

Next, draw a large circle anywhere you think it would be attractive on your design. Don't fill it in.

Now, make two smaller circles somewhere on your design. Don't fill them in, either.

All right. It's time to get out your crayons. Color in one of the small circles with a red crayon.

Color in the other small circle with a yellow crayon.

Finish your design by using two other colors of your own choice to fill in two other shapes.

A COMPLETED DESIGN WILL LOOK SOMETHING LIKE THIS. COLORS INDICATED BY THE SHADED AREAS.

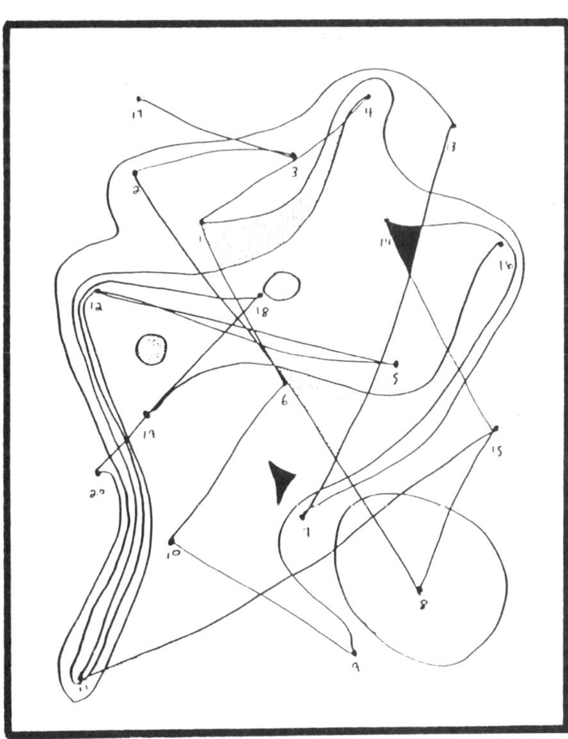

Build a Design (2)

About this activity...

More art! If you have ever taken a chemistry class, this design should remind you of a model of a molecular structure. Children will have fun with this project as they improve their listening and direction-following skills.

Materials needed...

Plain paper, pencil, crayons.

Directions to students...

We are going to do another "Build a Design" today, but by the time you are finished, this design is going to look very different from the first one you did. Let's get started.

- First, place your paper so that one of the short sides is closest to you.
- Now, using a pencil, put 12 dots anywhere you wish. Scatter them out as far as you can. Use the whole sheet of paper.
- Next, make 10 straight lines between the dots, making sure every dot is touched by at least one line. Since you are not using a ruler, don't worry if your lines aren't perfectly straight. It's okay if your lines cross each other.
- Now, make 10 more straight lines between the dots. They have to be new lines. It's okay to cross other lines for this part of the activity.
- Next, put a small circle — about the size of a pea — in every closed shape you have made.
- Now, draw straight lines to connect the circles. You may make as many lines as you wish, but you must make at least six.
- From here on, you'll be doing some coloring, so take out your crayons. (pause) Color every circle you have made red.
- Now, use your pencil again to make 10 more small circles. The circles have to be somewhere within the shapes you have drawn.
- Connect the new circles with as many straight lines as you want to make.
- Next, pick out any one color except red and color in the new circles.

- At this point, I want you to use your pencil again to make three small triangles. Put them wherever you think they need to go to make the design more interesting. They should not be touching any other lines.
- Next, using your pencil, draw straight lines to connect each triangle to any two circles.
- Pick out one more color you haven't used and color in the triangles.

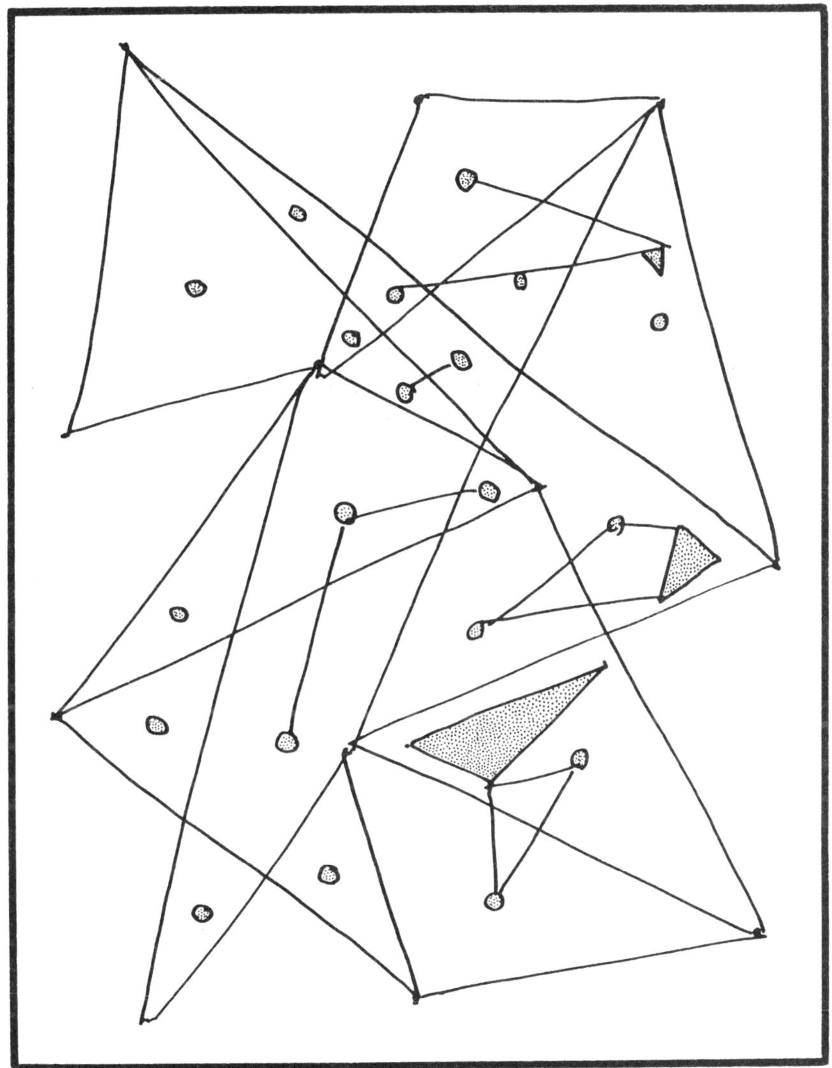

A FINISHED DESIGN. COLORED AREAS ARE INDICATED BY TONE.

Build a Design (3)

About this activity...

Every line in this design must be curved. As a result, it should suggest the kind of movement associated with music or dance.

Materials needed...

Plain paper, pencil.

Directions to students...

Today, we are going to do another "Build a Design" activity. I'm going to be giving you some directions which I want you to follow carefully.

First, place your paper so that one of the short sides is closest to you. Now, using your pencil, make 12 dots anywhere you wish, but scatter them out across the paper. Number the dots 1-12. It doesn't matter which dot gets which number. Remember to make your numbers small and to put them under the dots.

There are two rules you will be following for the first parts of this activity. They are: Every line you make has to be curved in some way, and you may not cross other lines.

Are you ready?

For this first set of directions, I want you to make your lines very dark. Remember, they must be curved.

Here we go.

- Connect Dots 1 and 7.
- Connect Dots 2 and 3.
- Connect Dots 4 and 11.
- Connect Dots 5 and 9.
- Connect Dots 8 and 12.
- Connect Dots 6 and 10.

Now, I want you to make five more curved lines. But this time, make your lines rather faint. Remember, the lines you make now cannot cross any of the dark lines you just made.

- Connect Dots 1 and 6.
- Connect Dots 2 and 7.
- Connect Dots 5 and 11.
- Connect Dots 4 and 8.
- Connect Dots 3 and 10.
- Connect Dots 9 and 12.

Next, we're going to make three more lines that are very dark. Your lines must still be curved, but this time they may cross other lines.

- Connect Dots 2 and 12.
- Connect Dots 4 and 11.
- Connect Dots 6 and 9.

Surprise! Now I want you to turn your design sideways. It looks a lot different, doesn't it? For the last part of the activity we will be looking at the design in this new way, so put your name in the bottom right-hand corner.

Your final job is to make one more line. It has to be curved. It can be light or dark, but it must start at one number and stop at a different number. Put the line where you think it should go to make your design more interesting and to give it a more balanced look.

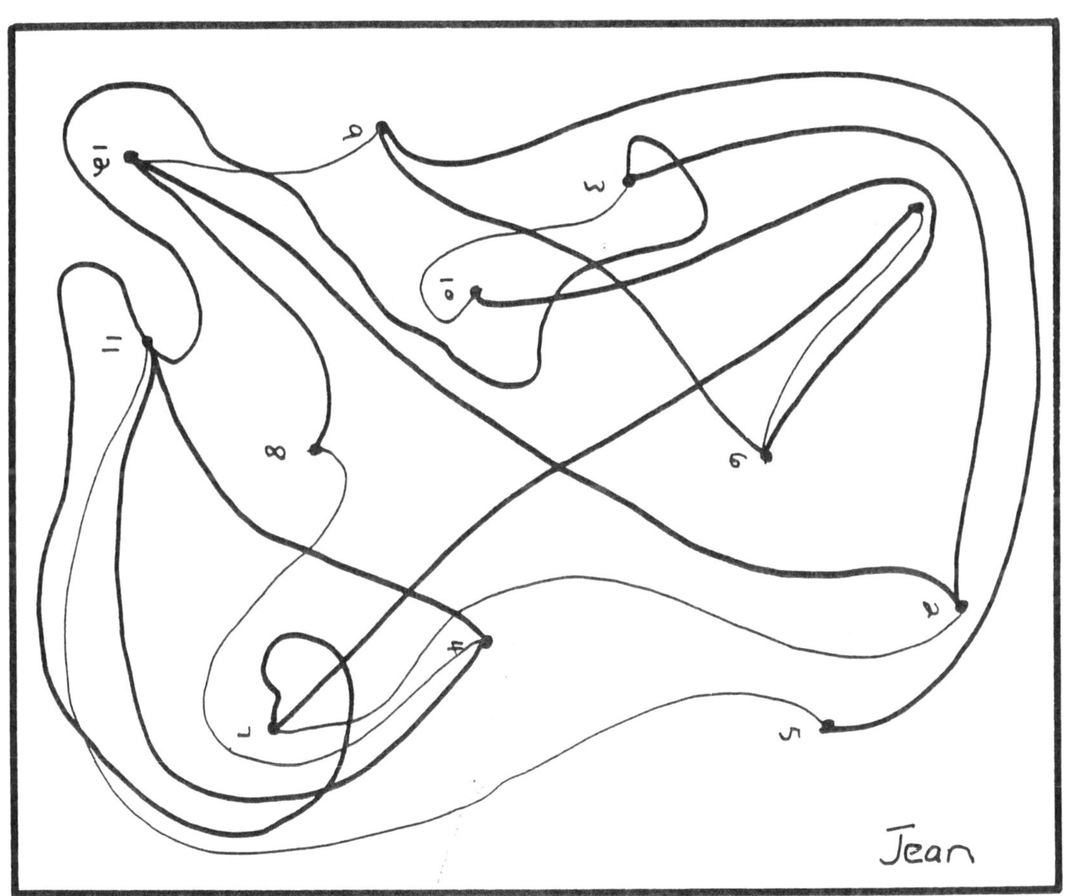

A FINISHED DESIGN (TURNED ON ITS SIDE AS DIRECTED). NOTE THAT ALL LINES ARE CURVED.

Build a Design (4)

About this activity...

This activity will produce a design with a linear look. Even though students are given certain directions which they must follow, the final look of the design will depend on a number of decisions which they are free to make as they move from step to step.

Materials needed...

Plain paper, pencil.

Directions to students...

We are going to do another "Build a Design" activity today, but this time we will be starting in an entirely new way. Instead of starting with dots, as we have done before, let's begin the design by drawing some lines.

- First, place your paper so that one of the short sides is closest to you.
- Now, using your pencil, I want you to draw five lines, but don't draw them until I've told you what to do. The lines you draw should be as straight as you can make them by hand (without a ruler). Each line should be of a different length, and you may place them anywhere you wish on the paper. They should not touch each other in any way. Go ahead and draw your five lines.
- Next, draw a straight line made up of dashes which crosses three of the lines you have already made.
- Now, draw a straight line made up of a lot of little circles which crosses two of the lines you have already made.
- Your next line should be jagged — like a lot of little v's put together. It should go in a straight direction, and should cross two of the first five lines you made. Do not cross any other lines.
- Your next line should be wiggly. It should look like waves, and should go in a straight direction. It should cross any three lines which you have made.
- Next, I want you to make three short, straight lines which do not cross or touch any other lines.
- Now, make three circles. Each of the circles should be about as big as a penny, and must not touch any of the lines you have made.
- Put a dot in the middle of each of the three circles.
- Next, draw a straight line between any two of the dots you just made.
- Here is your last job. Starting with the one dot which you did not connect, draw a straight line from that dot to the end of any one of the lines you have made.

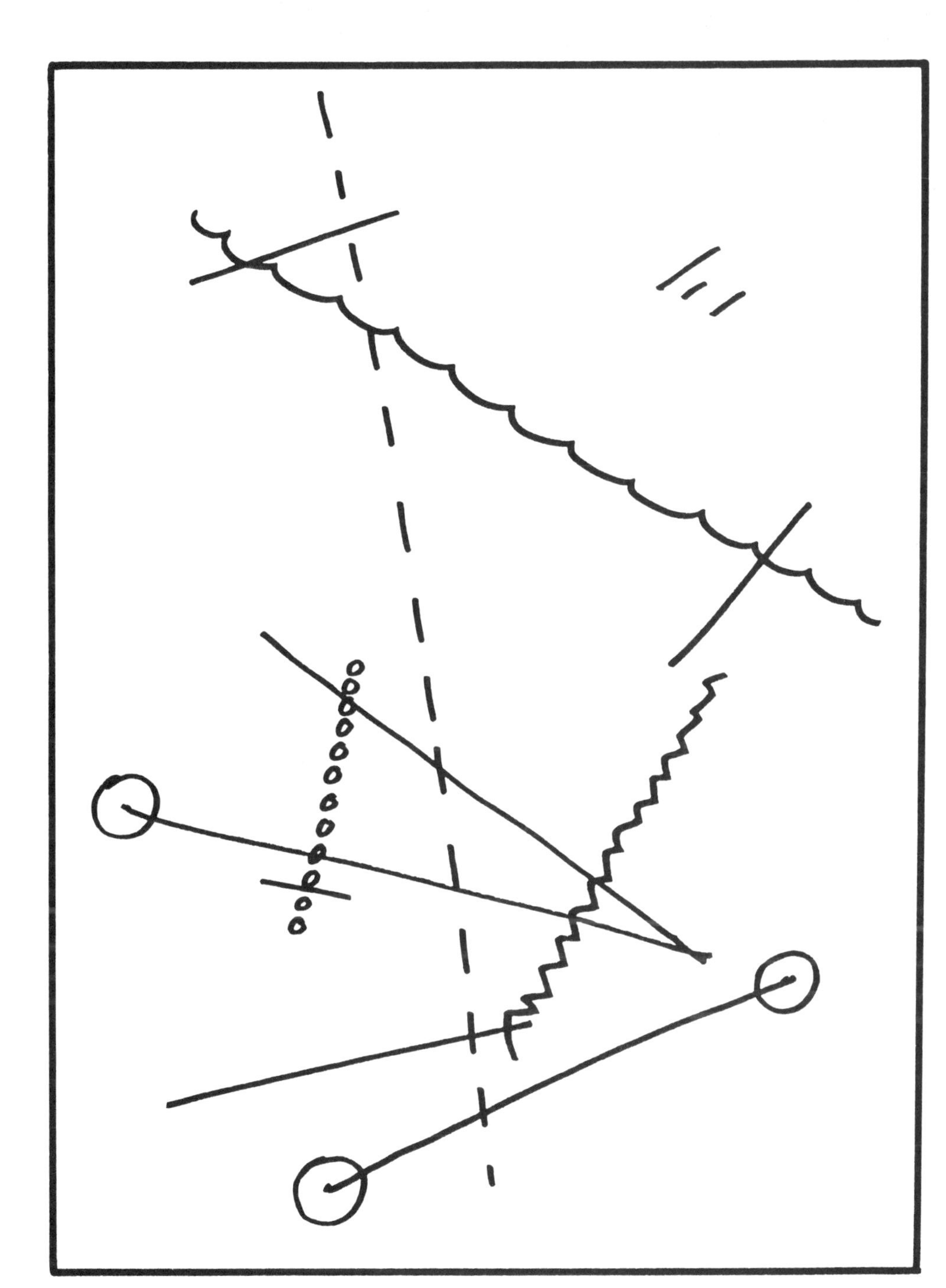

THIS ASSIGNMENT IS SO OPEN-ENDED THAT EVERY VERSION YOU SEE WILL BE DIFFERENT.

Grow Some Flowers

About this activity...

This activity is not as simple as it seems. To turn two number "8's" into a flower blossom requires a rather high level of conceptual ability.

Materials needed...

Worksheet (see illustration), pencil.

Directions to students...

Today, we're going to do an activity that should cheer everyone up. We're going to "grow" some flowers!

Take a look at the piece of paper I have given you. Notice that there is a long line and that there are five shorter lines. We're going to pretend that the long line is the ground, and that each of the shorter lines is the stem of a flower. I will be giving you a number of directions to follow. If you listen carefully and do as I say, you should end up with five very interesting flowers.

Are you ready? All right, first place your paper so that the long line is closest to you. Then, starting on the left, number the up-and-down lines 1-5. Put the numbers below the line that stands for the ground.

Now, it's time for the flowers!

- First, make a circle about as big around as your thumb is wide at the very top of Line 4.
- The next circle you make should be about half as big as the one you just made. It should be put a little bit above Line 2.
- Put a capital letter "U" at the top of lines 3 and 5. The "U's" should be about as wide as the big circle you drew at the top of Line 4.
- Draw a large number "8" at the top of Line 1. Make it about as high as the letter "U's" you just made.
- Next, give Flower 4 eight petals.
- Can you think of a way to use another number "8" to give Flower 1 a total of four petals? Try it.
- Give Flower 4 six long, pointed leaves.
- Give Flower 1 eight small leaves near the bottom of its stem.

- Can you think of any way to use a capital letter "W" to make Flower 5 look like a tulip? Here's a hint: How does the top edge of a tulip look?
- Did you know that there are really hundreds of different kinds of tulips? Let's turn Flower 3 into a tulip that has some interesting stripes on its petals.
- Now, give each tulip some leaves.
- I think Flower 2 could use some petals. Give it some very fluffy petals.
- Look! A bee has just landed on Flower 4. Draw it.
- Flower 2 has two very droopy leaves. Please draw them.
- Draw an ant crawling up the stem of Flower 1.
- Finally, let's give our flowers something they all need... some sunshine! Draw the sun anywhere you like, but try to put it in a place where you think it will look nice in your drawing.

THE WORKSHEET
USE 8½" x 11" PAPER.

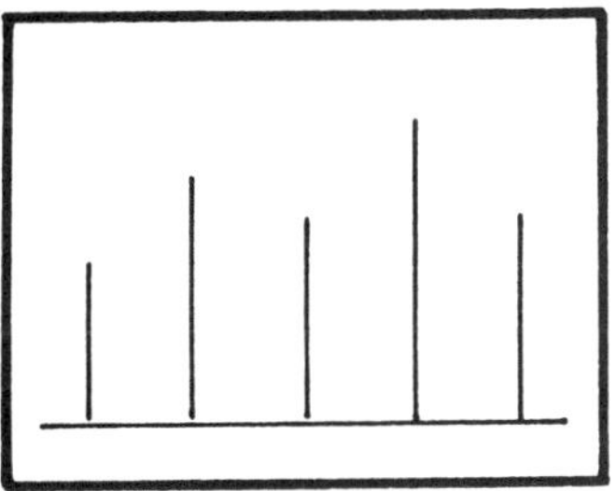

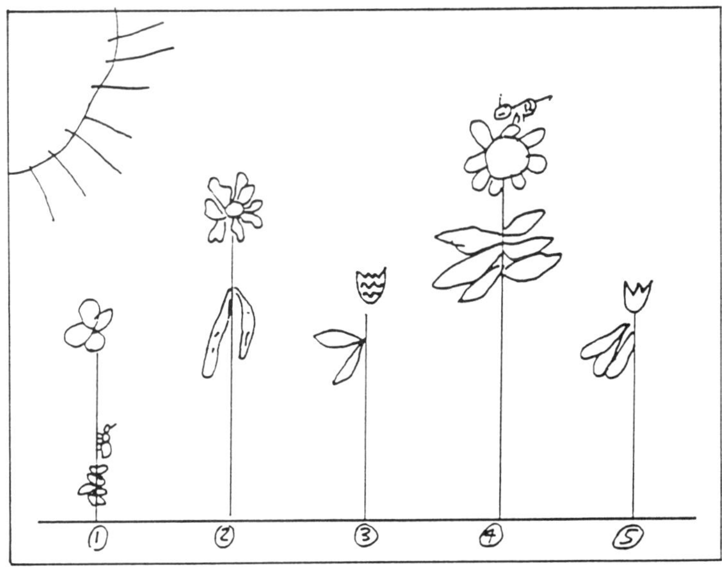

Michael Thompson, age 9

THE "FLOWER GARDEN."

Making a Mess

About this activity...

The title here is actually a little misleading because students must be quite meticulous in their tearing to do well with this activity. Your request that students remember what they have done will prove difficult.

Materials needed...

One piece of 3-hole notebook paper.

Directions to students...

Our direction-following activity today is called "Making a Mess." Do you think you can do that?

Here is what you will *not* need for this activity. You will not need a pencil, a ruler, scissors, crayons or anything else we normally use.

You *will* need the piece of notebook paper I have given you, and one other thing... I mean two other things... your hands. Did you bring them today?

Now, I am going to give you a long list of directions, and I want you to listen very carefully. Everything I ask you to do will have something to do with the piece of paper I have given you. Are you ready?

- First, pick up your paper very carefully so that you don't bend it or mess it up in any way.
- Now, when I say "go," I want you to crumple the paper into the smallest little ball you can. Get ready, get set, GO!
- Great. Now, open up your paper without tearing it and smooth it out.
- Now, crumple it again.
- Open it up and smooth it out again.
- Do the same thing two more times. Make sure you don't tear the paper.
- Now, fold your paper in half. Keep folding it in half until you can't make any more folds.
- Open up your paper and smooth it out.
- Now, roll your paper into a tube.
- Flatten the tube and fold it as many times as you can.
- Open up your paper and smooth it out.

- Now, make one more ball. Make it as tight as you can.
- Open up your paper and smooth it out.
- Next, I want you to tear all the way along the up-and-down line which is next to the holes. Tear off a long, thin strip, and try not to tear into the holes.
- Crumple the strip you just made into a little ball and set it aside.
- Now, tear another narrow strip from *each* of the other three untorn sides. Make your tears as straight as you can.
- Crumple the three strips of paper you have just torn into one ball and put the ball next to the crumpled strip that has the holes.
- Our piece of paper is getting smaller, isn't it? Well, let's make it a little smaller still. Tear another strip from one of the long sides. Make your strip wide enough so that you can tear it all the way off in one long strip without ripping it. Don't crumple it up yet.
- Now, how many letters are there in your first name? I want you to tear the strip you just made into that many pieces. If your name has four letters, for example, make four pieces.
- Crumple those little pieces into a ball if you can. If the pieces keep falling apart, just put them all together in a pile.
- Next, fold the piece of paper that is left in half along the long side. Press down to make the fold as sharp as you can.
- Now, rip the paper along the fold you just made. You don't have to do it perfectly, but try to end up with two pieces of about the same size.
- What's next? Crumple one of the two pieces you just made into a little ball. Put it with the other paper balls.
- Now comes the hardest part. Maybe it won't be so hard... we'll see.
- First, pick up the last "un-crumpled" piece. Now, think back over all of the instructions I have given you. How many separate pieces of paper do you think there are in your "scrap" pile? When you think you know, tear the piece of paper you are holding into that number of pieces.

  If you can't remember, just take a guess. That's okay. All right, do it now. The pieces you tear don't have to be the same size, by the way.
- After you have finished tearing, open up your paper wads as carefully as you can and count them to see if you were correct.

Letters and Rhymes

About this activity...

This activity is harder than it looks because each of these short poems contains several pieces of information which children must assimilate and then turn into a drawing. You may have to repeat some of the lines more than twice.

Materials needed...

Worksheet (see illustration), pencil.

Directions to students...

We are now going to do an activity called "Letters and Rhymes."

I am going to read 16 little poems. The poems all have something to do with letters of the alphabet. I will read each poem two times. Your job will be to listen to what is being described in the poem, and then to make a little drawing which shows what the alphabet letters are doing.

I have given you a piece of paper with 16 little boxes. Before we start, I want you to number the boxes 1-16, starting at the top left-hand box and going from left to right, row by row. Make your numbers small, and put them in the lower left-hand corner of each box.

Are you ready? We'll start with Poem 1. Make your drawing in Box 1.

1. I saw a little mouse
   Who found a place to hide
   Beneath a letter "K"
   Turned over on its side.

2. I saw a hungry fish
   With a mouth shaped like a "C."
   It was about to catch
   A swimming letter "D."

3. I saw a snake whose shape
   Was like "S's" end to end.
   It was wearing a big smile,
   So I guess it was a friend.

4. I saw a funny owl
   With letter "O's" for eyes.
   Its beak was like a "V,"
   And it really looked quite wise.

5. I saw a little kitten
   With a tail shaped like a "C."
   It was having fun
   Sitting on a "T."

6. I saw a little man
   Whose hair was quite a mess.
   And every hair he had
   Looked like the letter "S."

7. I saw two "D's" turned over
   To form two turtle shells.
   The turtles both were walking
   On legs like letter "L's."

8. I saw a funny face
   With a big "L" for a nose.
   The mouth looked like a "U,"
   And the eyes were made of "O's."

9. I saw an alligator
With looks so fierce they'd trouble you.
It had short legs and little eyes
And teeth like "M" and "W."

10. I saw a two-humped camel
With a big "M" for a back.
It was walking near
A little railroad track.

11. I saw a lady in a hat
Like a "U" turned upside down.
The hat was very tight,
And it made the lady frown.

12. I saw an elephant
Standing on some hay.
Its ear looked like a "C,"
And its trunk, a backwards "J."

13. I saw a spotted bug
With a body made of "O's."
It had long, skinny legs,
And feet with many toes.

14. I saw a happy clown
With a big "A" for a hat.
It had a funny collar,
And a nose that was quite fat.

15. I saw a pretty flower
With petals made of "V's."
It had a crooked stem
And leaves like "C's" and "D's."

16. I saw a little chair
Made from the letter "L."
It had letter "I's" for legs,
And was really made quite well.

Sadie Boge, age 10

THIS WORKSHEET MAY BE USED FOR THE "SHAPES AND RHYMES" ACTIVITY, ALSO.

Shapes and Rhymes

About this activity...

Don't let children get too self-conscious about the accuracy of their drawings. Stress that you are after "idea" drawings, not "art."

Materials needed...

Worksheet (see illustration), pencil.

Directions to students...

Our activity today is called "Shapes and Rhymes."

I am going to read 16 short poems. The poems are about the adventures of some shapes and lines. I will read each poem twice. Then, it will be your job to make a quick drawing that shows what is happening in the poem.

I have given you a piece of paper with 16 little boxes, one for each poem. Please number the boxes 1-16, starting at the top left-hand box and going from left to right, row by row. Make your numbers small, and put them in the lower left-hand corner of each box.

Are you ready? Then, we'll start with the first poem. Put your drawing in Box 1. Then, use Box 2 for the second poem, Box 3 for the third poem, and so forth.

1. Six little dots
   Went outside to play.
   All but one climbed up
   A giant letter "A."

2. Once upon a time,
   A shape with one curved side
   Took a pair of circles
   For a little ride.

3. I saw a wiggly shape
   That was very fat
   Sit down upon a circle
   And nearly squash it flat.

4. A square sat down
   On a circle and cried.
   Someone had taken
   A line from its side!

5. Once a little circle
   Met a little square.
   The circle had a beard.
   The square? It had long hair.

6. One day a hungry circle
   Ate some little dots.
   How many did it eat?
   It ate lots and lots.

7. Said the circle to the square
   "Now, please don't laugh.
   But as you can see,
   I've been cut in half."

8. Once a little circle
   Wearing many dots
   Climbed up on a square
   Covered with big spots.

9. Three little circles
Decided to sit down.
They sat down on a square,
Which wore a great big frown.

10. Once a happy circle
With a great big grin
Met a sad rectangle
Which was very thin.

11. Once a curvy line
Made up of dots and dashes
Met a line that looked
Like lightning when it flashes.

12. A tall, straight-sided shape
With a stripe across its middle
Found a hat and tried it on,
But it was too little.

13. Once a playful circle
Decided to have fun.
So it grew a pair of wings
And flew up toward the sun.

14. A circle and a line
Had an accident.
The circle's side was broken
And the line was bent.

15. Once I saw three circles
(All of them were lumpy)
Sitting on three squares
(All of them were grumpy).

16. A very clever circle
Performed a trick quite neat.
It grew arms and legs and hands
And tiny little feet.

Sadie Boge, age 10

Mystery Patterns

About this activity...

This activity asks students to build up a complicated pattern from simple, step-by-step directions. The design they make will not be perfect because no measuring is involved. However, use of a ruler for straight lines does give students enough control to do a good job.

Materials needed...

Worksheet (see illustration), pencil, ruler.

Directions to students...

I have given you a piece of paper which is blank except for four letters — A, B, C, and D. What are the letters for? Well, you'll have to wait and see. But I will give you this one hint: They are going to be the beginning of an interesting "Mystery Pattern."

First, I want you to take out a pencil and your ruler.

Next, make sure the C-D end of the paper is closest to you. You can turn the paper any way you wish as you do your work, but always bring it back to its original position — with the C-D end toward you — after you finish following each group of instructions.

Let's start.

- First, I want you to use your ruler and pencil to draw a straight line between the middle of letter A and the middle of letter D. Draw your line dark enough so you can see it easily.
- Next, connect the letters B and C with a straight line. (From now on, every time I tell you to connect two letters, I want you to use your ruler, okay?)
- Now, connect A and B, (pause) C and D, (pause) B and D, (pause) and A and C.

What shapes have we made so far? Yes, a square and four triangles.

- Next, using capital letters about as big as those that I made on your paper, put an E in the middle of the top triangle. (pause) Put an F in the middle of the bottom triangle. (pause) Put a G in the middle of the left-hand triangle. (pause) Put an H in the middle of the right-hand triangle.
- Now, draw straight lines between the following letters: E and H, (pause) G and F, (pause) G and E, (pause) and F and H.

Things are starting to get interesting, aren't they? Let's keep working.

- Connect these letters: A and E, (pause) B and E, (pause) A and G, (pause) B and H, (pause) C and G, (pause) C and F, (pause) D and H, (pause) and D and F.

Look! Now, we have made an attractive four-pointed star. Let's go ahead and draw some more lines to make it even more interesting.

- Connect these letters: A and H, (pause) A and F, (pause) B and G, (pause) B and F, (pause) D and G, (pause) D and E, (pause) C and E, (pause) and C and H.

Now, look what has happened. We have drawn lots of lines, but everything is still balanced, isn't it? There are really only two more lines we can draw and still keep our design completely balanced. Does anyone know what they are? (discuss) Okay, let's go ahead and draw them.

- Connect E and F, (pause) and G and H.

If you followed directions carefully, your designs should all look about the same. Let's see how you did.

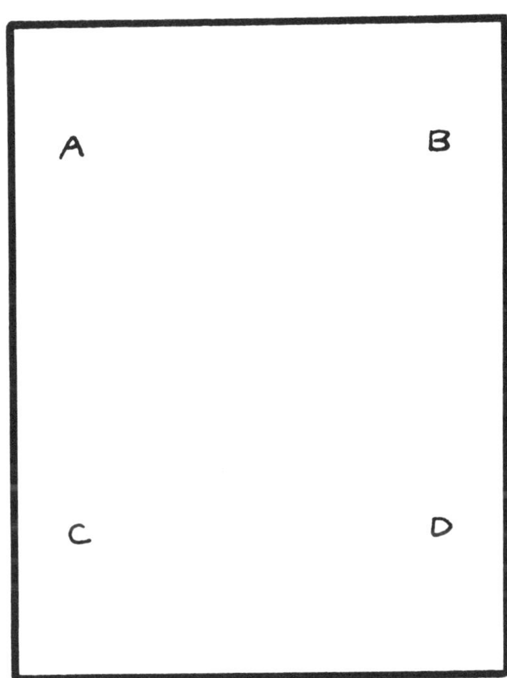

PROVIDE THIS WORKSHEET. BE SURE TO PLACE THE LETTERS IN A SQUARE PATTERN.

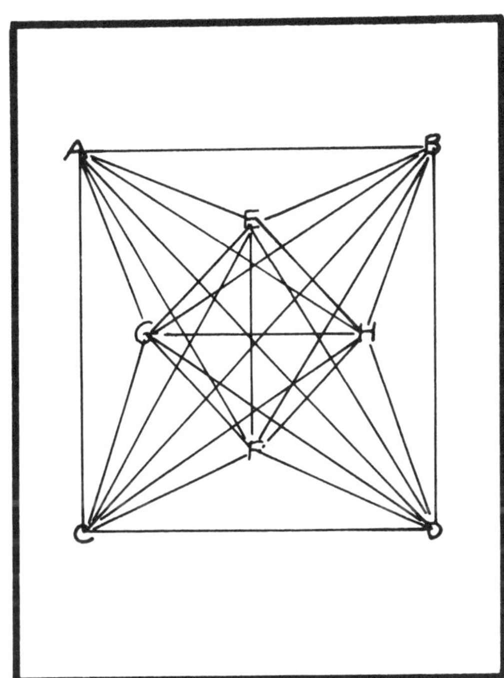

EXAMPLE OF A FINISHED "MYSTERY PATTERN."

Mystery Patterns (2)

About this activity...

Here, the activity starts with a circle and a square which you provide. Children will construct a symmetrical pattern that looks much like a traditional quilt block.

Materials needed...

Worksheet (see illustration), pencil, ruler.

Directions to students...

Today, we're going to make another interesting design. You will remember that last time we started with just four letters. This time, your "Mystery Pattern" starts with two shapes — a circle and a square.

You will need a pencil and ruler for this assignment. Get them ready now. Also, before we begin, be sure one of the short sides of the paper is closest to you. Now, listen very carefully.

- First, find the place where the circle touches the square at the top. Put a capital letter "A" right on top of that spot. Don't make it too large, but be sure to make it dark enough so that you can see it easily.

- Now, go to the bottom. Put a capital letter "B" on the place where the circle touches the bottom side of the square.

- Next, put the letter "C" at the place where the circle touches the square on the left-hand side, (pause) and the letter "D" where it touches the square on the right-hand side. Do you have that? You should have an "A" at the top, a "B" at the bottom, a "C" on the left, and a "D" on the right.

Now, we have all the points we need to make another square, don't we? Let's do it. Remember, use your ruler every time you make a line.

- Connect A and C, (pause) A and D, (pause) B and C, (pause) and B and D.

I guess we've really made a diamond shape, haven't we? All right. Let's keep going.

- Connect A and B, (pause) and C and D.

Next, we're going to do some measuring, but we're going to use our eyes rather than our rulers. Here's what to do.

- Look at the line between A and C. Halfway along that line — right on the line — put the letter E.

- Find the line between A and D. Put an F at the halfway point on that line.

- Put a G halfway between the B and the C, (pause) and an H halfway between the B and the D.

Do you have it? Now, let's do some more connecting.

- Make a line between E and F, (pause) between F and H, (pause) H and G, (pause) and G and E. Look! Another square!

There are all sorts of things we could do now, but let's start by connecting these letters:

- Connect E and H, (pause) and F and G.

Shall we go on? Okay, connect these letters:

- Connect A and G, (pause) A and H, (pause) B and E, (pause) B and F, (pause) C and F, (pause) C and H, (pause) D and E, (pause) and D and G.

You have made a very complicated design, haven't you? Since you didn't measure with a ruler, your design won't be perfect, but it should be very nice. Let's see how you did.

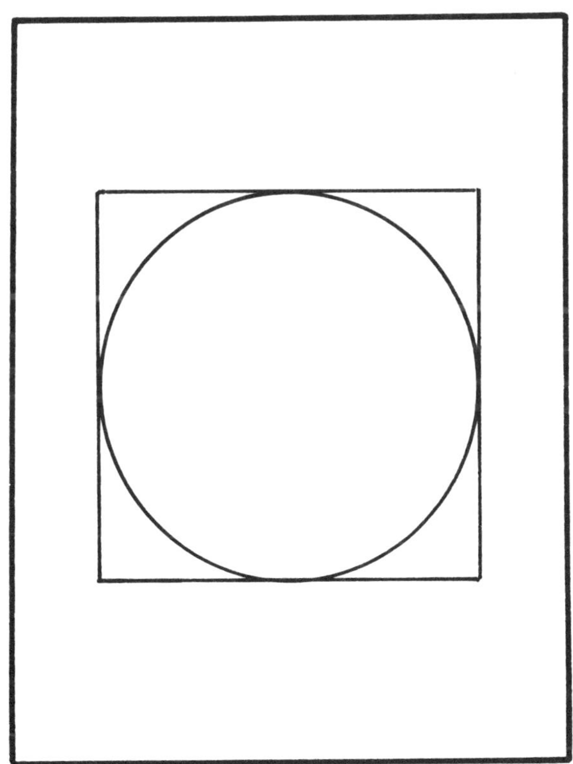

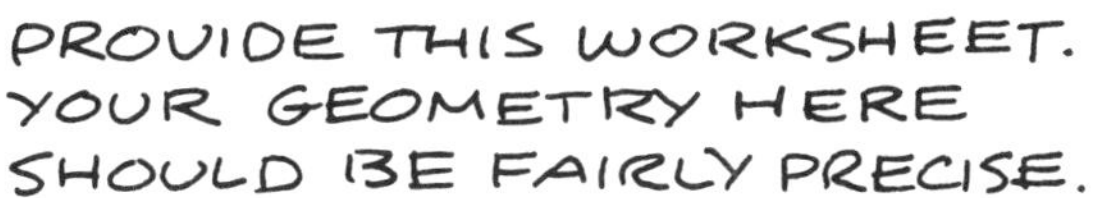

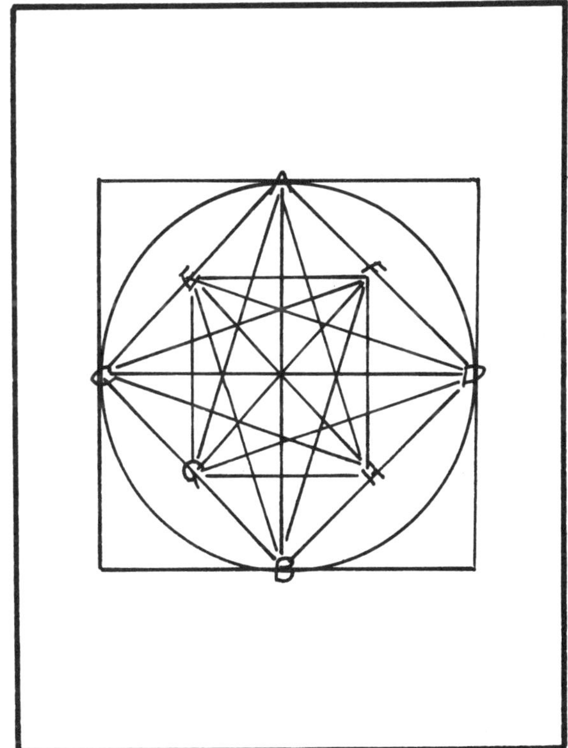

FINISHED "MYSTERY PATTERN"

Index

Publications by Tin Man Press

Is It Friday Already? Learning Centers That Work – 30 weeks of centers in nine subject areas.

Are They Thinking? – A comprehensive, year-long thinking skills program.

Loosen Up! – Art activities designed to build confidence.

T is for Think – More than 300 drawings spur thinking excitement.

OPQ – Offbeat Adventures with the Alphabet – A center approach based on the alphabet.

Waiting for Lunch – Sponge activities for those little moments in the day.

Great Unbored Bulletin Board Books I and II – 20 great board ideas in each book.

Great Unbored Blackboard Book – Quick analytical activities you do on the board.

WakerUppers – 50 friendly hand-drawn reproducible sheets to motivate thinking.

Nifty Fifty – 500 provocative questions about 50 everyday things.

Smart Snips – Each of the 50 reproducible activities starts with something to cut.

Ideas To Go – 50 different assignments cover a broad range of thinking skills.

Brain Stations – 50 easy-to-make centers promote creative and flexible thinking.

Play by the Rules – 50 scripted challenges turn students into better listeners.

The Discover! Series – 24 card sets provide hands-on experiences with everyday objects.

Adventures of a Dot Series – 10 card sets use a Dot character to encourage thinking.

Linework – Jumbo card set centers around the concept of line.

An Alphabet You've Never Met – Jumbo card set plays creatively with letters.

Going Places – Students participate in five interesting imaginary adventures.

Letter Getters – Letter clues encourage language development and deductive thinking.